MEMOIRS
of an ADOPTED
CHILD

THOMAS F. LIOTTI

MEMOIRS OF AN ADOPTED CHILD

iUniverse books may be ordered through booksellers or by contacting:

iUniverse
1663 Liberty Drive
Bloomington, IN 47403
www.iuniverse.com
844-349-9409

ISBN: 978-1-6632-1135-4 (sc)
ISBN: 978-1-6632-1133-0 (hc)
ISBN: 978-1-6632-1134-7 (e)

Library of Congress Control Number: 2020920253

Print information available on the last page.

iUniverse rev. date: 11/10/2020

This book is dedicated to both my newly discovered family and those that revealed them to me. My deepest gratitude is extended to Francesca, Mary, Eileen and my new family.

Acknowledgments

THE WRITING OF a book takes a tremendous amount of effort to express your inner most feelings and reveal the experiences that will capture the reader's attention. When writing non-fiction truth and accuracy are paramount in order to paint the vivid images that will visually take you on a journey through the book. This often requires the invaluable assistance of some incredible people who made this journey possible.

I would like to take the opportunity to express my heartfelt thanks to my daughter, Francesca Eileen, who gave me more than a birthday gift of Ancestry but assisted in the discovery of my roots which were unknown to me. While adoptees may be influenced genetically by their biological family, they are similarly influenced by the adoptive family's traditions, their living conditions, their learning choices and the attributes of their adoptive parents. With this in mind the adopted child, being a combination of both, is now a free agent to explore unchartered territories.

Francesca presented the key that opened the door and Mary Sirchia, a long lost cousin, walked through it. I am grateful that due to their efforts I now have knowledge of my biological family and the stability associated with it. I am a missing link entering into a new family which has always existed and who have accepted me with love. I am interested in the lives of each one of them because I did not live through their histories and experiences as they happened. I have to be gentle as I learn about them after the fact as it may be that some of those experiences are too hurtful for them to recall. My life like some of theirs' is no doubt filled with mistakes but they are forgiven because we are family.

I must also acknowledge Rosemary Ellerby, my Law Office Manager, who initially accepted the call from Mary Sirchia and was told of her amazing discovery. Rosemary is the filter who screens some of my calls and instantly gave Mary and her discovery, credibility. That was the beginning of the miraculous breakthrough that ended my 10-year quest to find my biological family. Whatever other amazing feats that Mary has had in her life, this should be near the top of the list.

It was Rosemary and Liliia Salakhutdinova, a brilliant Paralegal in my Law Office who have piloted this book to fruition. Like all books it has gone through multiple drafts, editing, formatting, spell checks, layouts, book cover design and more. Rosemary and Liliia are responsible for the finishing touches and presenting the book for publication.

Introduction

SOME TIME PASSED before I was able to collect my thoughts and write this book. It is a sequel to *The Secret Adoption*, (iUniverse, 2011). This book contains memories of my life. *Memoirs of an Adopted Child* is full of unforeseeable circumstances and gripping discoveries. It shows that if you are persistent and passionate about something, great results may await you.

The heartbreak of losing two adoptive parents and any attempt to discover my biological origin at 60 years of age was emotionally devastating. Many years would pass contemplating my adoption and how to discover my roots when my daughter, Francesca, presented me with a gift whose value would not be revealed for a considerable time after it was received. It was an Ancestry Kit that prompted Mary Sirchia, while searching her own family tree, to ascertain she was my second cousin. Mary opened the door for communication and life changing events.

The journey that I started after finishing my first book culminated with the discovery of my biological parents followed by a reunion with my cousins, nieces, nephews and their extended families. The meeting afforded me a warm and loving welcome from my new family who embraced me with open arms.

Chapter I

The Search

(Chapter XXII from The Secret Adoption)

AFTER BEING TOLD at age 60 that I was adopted, my thoughts turned to whether I should bother to unravel this mystery. I had simultaneous feelings of bewilderment at my sudden loss of a base, a sense of betrayal at not being told and isolation or alienation. But it also awakened a curiosity about myself, my own limits and potential. It gave me an identity with other orphans, wards of the state, outcasts, bastards and others left with no more than swaddling clothes for their heritage. It occurred to me that since the Catholic Church did not decide that Mary was a virgin until 400 A.D. that Mary and Joseph might have been adoptive parents of Jesus.

But what was my heritage in this life or others? I was starting at ground zero. Friends told me, what difference does it make, you are who you are, and you have your own identity? That is fortifying, a badge of courage and honor. Where others have had the reinforcement of blood kin, role models, successful siblings to emulate, I had only myself. I did not have a compass or other navigational tools to take me back to my past.

After reading a book given to me by my daughter Francesca on reincarnation therapy, I became more curious about previous lives as an alternative. I was not necessarily a believer, but felt that there was more to this life than meets the eye. There is far too much in the way of ancient beliefs and the science of astrology to entirely discount parapsychology, the supernatural and reincarnation. It gave me hope whereas the other side of the coin was saying when you are dead, you are dead, and there is no heaven, hell and purgatory. On the later, you either passed life's SAT exam or you did not.

The meaning of life or what is known, stands in contrast to the meaning of death, which is unknown. We have set up a reward system for ourselves where the good that we accomplish in this life will give us entrance into the next. Somewhere out there the great book of your life and all others is kept, or, is it?

This life is supposed to give us eternal life in heaven where we will be reunited with those we have loved. This makes death easier to accept. While my father Louis was a brilliant, open minded person, he was also an ardent Catholic who often said to me: "Faith is the greatest thing in this life." While I would love to be reunited with my adoptive parents so that I could tell them of how much their love for each other and me has meant to me, I do not have that faith. I regret not having embraced them and not tearfully telling them of how grateful I am for their total devotion to me throughout their lives. They truly gave me their all. They sacrificed their entire lives for me.

After my adoptive parents, Louis and Eileen, passed away, I was lost. Gripped by my own bereavement, angry at not being told sooner, yet I was glad that I had not been. My search for a connection to the past was enlivened by my own and my children's actual or potential health issues. This, by itself, seemed to be justification for exhuming the past of those who might prefer that it be forgotten. But for them and for me, it could never be. There is a gaping hole in the past which may never be filled.

I am glad that I was not told sooner because I did not have to deal with the rejection, loss of identity and negative aspect of knowing about my adoption. My existence and that of my adoptive parents was cloistered perhaps because their extended family knew of my adoption and my parents wanted to keep that as a secret from me. They no doubt worried that the revelation would cause me to reject them but I do not believe that that would have happened. Where would I go? I also think that my adoptive parents may have felt some banishment or rejection by society as a whole due to their inability to conceive a child of their own. That was the conventional thinking at the time, that there was something wrong with people, mentally or physically, if they could not conceive. Instead of appreciating the enormous self-sacrifice involved in adoption, society at large, at that time, looked down on adoptive parents and adoptive children. My adoptive parents spared me from all of those very negative conflicts.

Adoptive children were also looked down upon as different since society did not know of our origins and assumed the worst about natural parents who gave their children up for adoption – there must be something wrong with them or the child that is given up. We would not have measured up to society's norms at the time. My adoptive parents carried these burdens of thought and conscience with them for their entire lives but thankfully, saved me from it.

I arrived an hour early for my appointment scheduled for Sunday, July 19, 2009 at 12:15 p.m. I waited in my car, down the street, reading The New York Times, but having difficulty focusing on the articles, thinking of the unexpected experience that I would soon encounter, how My life had been radically altered by these developments. Uncertainties and self-doubt were comforted by my resolve in deliberately trying to uncover the past. I did not have anxiety but felt relief over the fact that I would pursue the search, somewhat prepared to accept wherever it may lead.

I told a friend at my beach club part of the story and she told me of a "channeler," a former Apostolic Priest who purportedly takes you back in your life and past lives. She asked if my mind was open to it. He communicates with the other side, with the dead. He does not describe this as a gift. Instead, he refers to himself as "a vehicle." The only information that he had about me beforehand was my date of birth.

I was led into a room in his immaculate suburban home where he cared for his elderly parents. Tom is a trim man perhaps fifty to fifty-five years of age, with jet black hair, thinning slightly at the rear. He was tanned with evidence of red, recent sunning on his face. He wore a blue short sleeved shirt, white shorts and white socks pulled up just below the mid-calf. He had no shoes and looked very comfortable.

In the room which I recall as windowless and painted white, I was told to sit on one side of a coffee table. In front of me on the table I saw an old-time tape recorder for the large, blank, sixty-minute cassette tape that I was told to bring with me and a small pile of very detailed, printed astrological charts. On one side of the room which was approximately ten by ten feet, I saw bookshelves with titles that I could not read. On the floor was a statue, two to two- and one-half feet in height of the Blessed Mother. On the other side of the table facing me was Tom's chair and behind him I saw a few religious artifacts such as some crosses and religious pictures of saints. None of this was distracting or intimidating. It blended in with the surroundings and what lay ahead of me.

He closed the door and left the room for a few minutes, telling me to get my tape ready. I was told to bring photos with me. They lay on the floor, face down.

He told me not to volunteer information, not to respond until he spoke to me or pointed his finger at me. He turned sideways in his chair. He looked at the birth dates of my children and my wife on his charts. His head was turned away from me. I could see his profile. His eyes were squinting. His eyelids were flickering. He started saying names and letters asking who they were. I complied wherever I could. After thirty minutes he said: "What is the first question you want answered today?" I only had one question. Who are my biological parents? He said my mother was a young girl. "She met an older man in Little Italy. She did not look like the other people there. He saw the name Kelly around her. At first, he thought that my father might be a restaurant owner or Maître d'. He is dead. My mother is still alive. He could have been a judge, a lawyer or politician. They had an affair. It was a scandal within my family. She was told by him that she had to give me up for adoption or he would ruin her life. His name may have been William L. _."

My adoptive father Louis was speaking to him. He is in heaven. He told me that Louis did not tell me the whole story. He lied. He is keeping the secret. He will not give it up. There was a meeting with Cardinal Hayes in 1946 about the adoption. My adoptive mother had two miscarriages during the War. I was told by my father that it was seven. When my father Louis told me that I was young. I cried at the loss of brothers and sisters that might have been. My reaction to the news may have stopped my father from telling me that I was adopted.

We spent some time talking about my family and I left it to him to decide whether we should meet again. He said he would have to pray over it. He asked me what I thought of his room. I told him that he was very sincere and credible. It was a powerful place where something very mystical was occurring. I was living the DaVinci Code. I was in the catacombs, below the Vatican where Popes are buried, unearthing the very secrets of life, possibly eternal life or simply just communicating with the great beyond.

I told him at the end of the meeting that I had my doubts as to whether there was an actual adoption. I told him that I felt that there may not be any papers on file. He agreed. In retrospect what he told me was in no way accurate but I still have respect for his attempted search into the great beyond.

Chapter II

Ethnic Pride

(Chapter XXIII from The Secret Adoption)

FOR MINORITIES WHO have felt the wrath of discrimination themselves or who have ancestors who were the victims of it, ethnic pride is often a justifiable response to prejudice. Each ethnic group advertises the successes of its members while they strive to take better positions in the hierarchy of the "melting pot." My adoptive parents raised me to respect all minorities and to have some resistance to authority. I have referred to it as an uneasy, symbiotic relationship with the establishment. My mother Eileen was of Scotch-Irish descent. Her father, Francis Lambe, was born in Glasgow, Scotland in circa 1880 and her mother, Anna Lambe, nee Burke, traced her ancestry to Dublin, Ireland, although she was born here in circa 1896. I do not know their exact dates of birth.

Certainly, I was reminded of the hard lives that the Irish had in assimilating into this country. They were able, through politics and because they were English speaking, to acquire a foothold in the New York City Police and Fire Departments. The Italians had a much more difficult time. They had darker skin tones and did not speak the language, but they were artisans, willing to work with their hands in construction. After all, they built the Roman Empire, Florence and Venice. Many who came to this country were from Calabria and southern Italy, the poorest part of Italy. They looked for advantages here that they did not have at home. Most were poor. A few unfortunately gravitated to organized crime, but most were hardworking and content to make their living the old-fashioned way, by working hard and earning it.

My mother endured all forms of discrimination even within her own family. One Irish relative remarking that my father was the only "guinea" he ever liked. My mother would wince at the word. It was unspeakable in our household as was any other ethnic slur. My father was willing to start a fight with anyone saying it or if he suspected that they were even thinking it. My mother was a vocal proponent of Italians. She had not an ounce of prejudice within her, neither did her father. My father admired both his father and her's.

When Lee Iacocca, the former Chairman of the Board of Chrysler Corporation championed the redevelopment of Ellis Island, establishing it as a historic landmark in 1986, my parents made sure that both of my grandfathers were enshrined in the Ellis Island Wall of Immigrants. When I first ran for political office, I became a member of the Irish American Society and the Ancient Order of Hibernians. I also joined the Sons of Italy in America and later other ethnic groups including the Columbian Lawyers' Association of Nassau County, Inc. where I eventually became their President and received their Distinguished Service Award. In the early days of my legal career, my father came to every legal meeting with me. He talked me up to Sal Spano, the Executive Director of the Association who got me started in the organization by making me an Officer in it. In 1993, I became a member of Tiro A Segno, the oldest ethnic club in the United States, Founded in 1880 and still located in three side by side townhouses at 77 MacDougal Street in Manhattan's Greenwich Village. My father paid my initiation fee there. He supported me in everything I ever did. He was a model of what a good parent should be. He placed my mother first and she placed me first.

My mother could not have children, perhaps because of her medical condition of Epilepsy. But my father was smitten with love to the core of his being, ever protective of my mother, loyal to her in every way. As I grew up there was more emphasis placed on my Italian heritage than my Scotch/Irish background. Having a new family that is predominantly Irish is forcing me into a different way of prideful thinking about the Irish. I am proud to be both Irish and English and having been raised as an Italian.

Chapter III

At Least One Sibling

(Chapter XXIV from The Secret Adoption)

IN A DECISION by Surrogate Judge Riordan on December 14, 2009, I learned that my natural mother had another child at the time of my birth. I do not know if I have a half brother or sister. If alive, they would be older. I was trying to determine what an encounter with them would be like, the awkwardness of it. I am also trying to imagine what they might be like, how they were raised, what their life experience had been. My gut tells me that I probably do not want to know much about them; that it is unlikely that they could overcome my resistance to learn more about them. I might resent what they may know which I now seek to learn, my identity. Who am I? Where did I come from? What could they tell me about a mother, no a woman, who gave me up at birth, who deserted me? When she did that, did she think that she was giving me a better life or a worse one? What could cause a woman to give up a child that has grown inside of her, to whom she has given birth? Was I simply a burden or were there circumstances that required it? Would she have aborted me if it were legal at the time? Did she give some thought to an illegal abortion or one out of the state or country? What would my life have been if I had been raised by my biological parents? I am grateful for all that I had. I do not imagine that I would have been raised on Park Avenue or gone to the best private schools had I been raised by my biological parents. Would I have been raised as an aristocrat, a member of the New York social elite? I doubt it if the superintendent of my parent's apartment building in Brooklyn knew of my pregnant mother's plight. Somehow, I do not think that my biological parents were close, personal friends with the Rockefellers or Brook Astor.

While I raise these questions about my mother, I have even more concern about my father. My mother did not do this by herself. I cannot blame her alone for the circumstances that gave rise to my birth and adoption. She perhaps recognized her own limits in not being able to care for me. But my father, now that is another story. What responsibility, if any, did he assume? Did he stand tall with honor and dignity by supporting my mother or did he abandon her as many men do, leaving my mother to fend for herself? Did he even know she was pregnant? Did she tell him? Was she able to tell him? Did she know who he was? What did she know about him?

In the final analysis, I would blame my father if it is determined that he mistreated or abandoned the woman who gave birth to me, not for his neglect of me alone. After all, what was I but a life, just a blob of flesh and bones, unable to speak or even walk. The burden that I presented was greater than the joy I might bring. So, I was not aborted. I had life. I would be a ward of the state, left in an orphanage or rescued by others who needed the joy I might bring, who would assume the responsibility for me, a stranger. They did not know my fate either, but they agreed to help to determine it.

Mary Sirchia has reminded me that we must not judge others. She is so right about that. None of us, regardless of our status in life, are in a position to judge others. Had it not been for my adoptive parents I might Have wound up in an orphanage like Babe Ruth; or been an alcoholic and gone to jail or been a homeless person. I was very lucky that Louis and Eileen took me in sight unseen. They gave me love which is all any child wants or needs. They were people of modest means but they gave me all that they could. I was spoiled but not privileged.

Chapter IV

The Search Continued

AT SIXTY I learned that I was adopted. That was thirteen years ago when my adoptive father who was a few months from death told me. He was angry at the time that he had to leave our home to go into assisted living and blurted out: "you're not my son." My adoptive mother had Alzheimer's. My adoptive father, Louis, died in April, 2008 and my adoptive mother, Eileen Frances, followed in August, 2008. I had almost no details of my biological parents but filed a motion to unseal my adoption file for medical reasons. The Surrogate Judge at that time agreed to it. The Court appointed a Law Guardian to review the file and recommend whether it should be opened. An investigator was hired who determined that my biological mother was deceased and my biological father was unknown but also probably dead since he was, according to records, forty-two when I was born in 1947 at Doctors Hospital in Brooklyn, New York.

I soon began my own search. I started to write a book which was published at the end of 2011, *The Secret Adoption* (iUniverse, 2011). My local newspaper and Newsday carried stories on the book which then generated more interest. The book is dedicated to my adoptive parents but when I began to write it, I had little information to go on about my natural parents. I was told by my adoptive father that had I not been adopted, I would have been an orphan, a "ward of the state." I was turned over to my adoptive parents, Louis J. and Eileen F. Liotti, within days of my birth. My reputed biological mother and they both lived in Brooklyn. Although they were not officially named as such and received nothing for my care, they remained my foster parents, albeit not officially, for four and one-half years until they moved to East Meadow, Long Island and officially adopted me in November, 1951. On those adoption papers, my biological mother was shown as Anne S. Ferguson Smith. My first birth certificate issued in 1947 carried my name as Donald Smith. She stated in those papers that she was unmarried when she had me. That was not correct, or so I thought in 2008. My investigator had located Anne Ferguson in Brooklyn. The Anne Ferguson he found was married to Harold Ferguson. Harold was born in 1907 and died in 1967. Anne was born in 1912 and died in 2000. I never met Anne or Harold during their lifetimes.

Anne and Harold moved to Port Washington, Long Island in 1962 residing at 10 Hawthorne Avenue. After the Newsday article appeared, a neighbor, Joan, from across the street from where the Fergusons had lived, wrote to me, at first to correct some of the dates appearing in the newspaper article but also informing me that the Fergusons had at least four children. Richard who was killed in Vietnam in 1968, Douglas who moved to Chicago and died sometime in the 1990's; Jim who lived in Ohio and Anne C. Ferguson who lived in Staten Island. I arranged for a meeting with Joan and another neighbor, Linda, at Joan's home. Joan moved into the community in 1968 and Linda has been there since her birth in 1941. Joan and Linda were both regal in their appearances, refined and highly articulate. Each showed a sincere interest in helping me to uncover the secrets of my biological mother's life.

Prior to meeting with Joan and Linda I checked the Nassau County land records and learned that the Fergusons' purchased their home in Port Washington in 1962. Following Harold's death Anne S. sold it in 1988. Thereafter she moved to Ohio to live with or near her son Jim. She died in Ohio but her body was brought back to New York to be buried with her husband Harold in the Nassau Knolls Cemetery in Port Washington. She was waked at a funeral home in Long Island.

An obituary appearing in the Port Washington News on February 25, 2000 revealed that Anne had other children including Robert and Susan, neither one was known to Joan and Linda but jogged their memories to the point where they remembered that Anne's mother had lived with her and that Anne's maiden name was Scott. Also, in that obituary were the names of two grandchildren.

Nassau Knolls Cemetery is an old grave yard with some of the markers pre-dating World War I. Walking through that grave yard in search of my mother's marker was a reflective experience where I was not emotional but taken with thoughts of the lives of others. I contemplated the staid normalcy, even the dullness and uneventful lives of my reputed biological mother except for the personal travails which she encountered. I considered my own birth and mortality as I thought of theirs'; so many lives which have come and gone with little to show for it except obscure grave markers, memories and the hopes or prayers of many that they will be reunited in the hereafter. Since I am an atheist, on the basis of present evidentiary facts, the prospect of rejoining in death provided little solace. At the same time, the moist graveyard ground over which I walked gave me a sinking feeling where I felt my own spirit or body going into the coffins below wondering if those or their remains have truly rested in peace or have, they or their spirits moved on to some other place, leaving nothing but the bones that they used while on earth. As we seek unification with others in life, we also search for that in death. Our search may end with our death but during our lives, that search continues.

By the time I had reached the cemetery the office was closed but the manager of the funeral home gave me a map of the area where she was buried. The area was called Colonial Gardens. I did not have a plot location but a vague description that the Gardens were just past the entrance and behind the Port Washington Police Station. I parked my car at the side of the narrow asphalt roadway, making my way on foot to the area that I believed to be Colonial Gardens. I walked along the rows of graves, perhaps two hundred yards long. The tombstones were back to back with perhaps eight rows on a hilly plateau going up at forty-five degrees. As I walked along the rows I had to look to my left and right to catch the names on both sides of me. I saw no other living persons on the chilly February day. I walked up and down for an hour and a half with no luck. Around me were grave markers, some new and some old; some with no names and broken crosses. These were the graves of persons long forgotten with family dead or gone. I thought of their spirits underground, their decaying bodies somehow still feeling whatever caused their deaths and longing for contact but left in a darkened, cold hole, with no human contact, just dirt all around them. They might be buried with or next to a loved one, each in their separate boxes. What comfort could there be in that unless it comes before death where you know that you will be buried next to your loved ones, together exploring the uncertainties of death?

I was getting ready to leave. I began to walk toward my car, when suddenly on the hill I noticed a grey headstone with the name Ferguson on it. There it was, larger than some of the others. On the left side of the stone as I faced it, the name Anne S. Ferguson was engraved. Harold's name appeared in the middle with Richard's name on the right. No one else's name appeared. There were unattended bushes on either side of the tombstone.

I stood before that grave marker for a few minutes trying to imagine what they looked like in life. Also, thinking that Richard, born in 1944, was killed in Vietnam. How lucky I was to be adopted. Had I not been, I might have wound up dead in Southeast Asia. In my book I wrote of how I avoided the draft in the 1960's. My adoptive father, Louis, fought valiantly in World War II but encouraged me to avoid military service. Richard reached the rank of Corporal, the same rank that my adoptive father held. But my adoptive father survived the Normandy invasion, promising his God that if he survived, he would say his rosary and go to church each day. That he did throughout his life until he was finally not able to get there anymore but saying his rosary for as long as he could even as he took nitro glycerin five times a day to thwart the angina pain. He kept his word and there was nobody who was tougher in life than he.

I then had to compare, by speculation, the Fergusons with the upbringing I received. I was apparently one of seven children that Anne had. Did the courage that she showed in having me and giving me up for adoption indicate her inner strength, a quality I too would like to possess? When she lied in the adoption papers to say that she was not married when I was born, was that for Harold's protection, mine or her own?

Alienation is a psychological term. The feeling of alienation implies a cause and effect, the exact cause being unknown. In the case of adoptees not told of their adoption until later in life, such as myself, the question is whether the cause is subconscious or whether it exists at all? Is alienation just something that is natural, that each of us feel at various times in our lives? Once told of adoption, does it add to the cumulative effect of alienation in those of us who are adopted? Does the revelation of being told exacerbate a pre-existing condition which may either be normal or exaggerated? In my case, I have determined that a sense of alienation or rejection has operated in me at the subconscious level for most of my life. This may be a cause of what psychologists would refer to as over compensation or the need for recognition of achievement as a sign of acceptance. A gregarious or outgoing personality which may seem self-centered or narcissistic or egomaniacal may also be explained by a heightened need for acceptance of who we are. A drunk acting out with obnoxious expressions may be in search of himself or perhaps he realizes that he has found that inner self and is displeased with his findings.

While it is certainly a stretch of the imagination but when I turned fifty, I told my wife that I wanted to go to England to visit the Inns of Court and Old Bailey, the Criminal Court. This was before I learned of my adoption but it occurred to me after I learned of it that subconsciously I may have had a longing to go there since my first birth certificate indicated that my biological father was English. When I mentioned this to my wife, she thought that was ridiculous but she was not adopted.

On the flip side of that is the fact that I am a criminal defense attorney, a very zealous one who supports the Declaration of Independence, the Constitution and the patriots who rebelled against King George during the Revolutionary War. But then again maybe it took the courage of the descendants of the English to fight against the English.

All of this may be pure coincidence and typical of anyone of my age and background but it does give me some pause to consider what the subconscious knows and what I might have remembered from my birth and infancy. Today parents read to their newborns in order to accelerate development. Maybe that works and maybe it does not but it might have worked on me without anyone intending or planning it. Could I have had an appreciation for my fate or somehow been privy to the events surrounding my adoption? When I was handed over to my adoptive parents, what was said and by whom? Was I turned over to my adoptive parents in the hospital? I have imagined nurses talking about how I was going to be orphaned and left behind. They are not in my brain knowing of the adoption. Instead, my brain tells me that my mother was discharged and that I was left behind.

I was born at Doctors Hospital in Brooklyn on May 29, 1947 and apparently turned over to my adoptive parents on June 6, 1947. But where was I for those seven or eight days? Was I delivered naturally or did my mother have a cesarean section? Was she convalescing in the hospital? Did she ever nurse me? If not, what affect did that have on my development, both physical and psychological?

Children who are not adopted may be more inclined to accept facts once they know them or simply to ignore them given other circumstantial evidence about their parenting. But adoption leads to unanswered questions. It is more than idle curiosity. It has to do with the inability to use deductive reasoning to fill in gaps of knowledge. Deductive reasoning can only work if you have operational facts from which to deduct. This is one of the problems created by the secrecy surrounding adoptions. Instead of answers, adoptees are often left with unanswered questions; questions that can never be answered. That is the frustration and even the cause of anger that brews in some of us. In 2019 New York passed legislation that now permits adoptees to get access to their adoption files which should include medical and other information but we are not there yet.

The American Psychiatric Association's Diagnostic and Statistical Manual for Mental Disorders (DSM-5) tells us that alienation in its most extreme form can be the antecedent for a psychosis, namely a departure from reality. That can be episodic or prolonged, even resulting in paranoidal schizophrenia, particularly if someone may already be genetically or chemically predisposed to that condition. Part of my adjustment throughout my life, subconsciously, and now consciously, is the realization that not every rejection need result in a feeling of alienation.

Yet as an only child without anchors to brothers and sisters with whom I might confide, there is a further detachment. I have been lucky that my subconscious alienation has never percolated into a psychosis. That is because each of us as long as we remain sane, monitor our behavior, we control it, repress certain feelings including alienation and delusions which can otherwise occur.

When I was young, pre-pubescent, my adoptive father told me that my adoptive mother had seven miscarriages. I cried over the brothers and sisters that I never had. Louis may have been on the verge of telling me of my adoption at that point, but may have backed off when he saw my distress. Although, very young at the time, the event stands out in my mind and I admired my mother for trying so hard to conceive. It showed me how important a child with my father was to her. My mother worked at showing my father that I was his real son. I would go with her every night when she could pick up my father at the train station when he was arriving home from work.

My mother knew that my father wanted a son to carry on the family name. it was a tribute to his father after whom I was named. I did everything with my father. When he came home from work, I would accompany him to his bedroom while he changed out of his business suit into more casual clothes. Then, we would go into the backyard and I would pitch to him before dinner. He taught me how to pitch, curve balls, side arms, submarines, fastballs, knuckleballs, and changeups. He made me into a Pony League All Star where I struck out the other side, nearly hit a home run and picked off a great player at first base. I did it to make him proud of me. He deserved it. He was the President of the League, so I had to prove that I was worthy of being an All-Star and that I did not get there due to any special treatment by him. I had to prove myself in his eyes and everyone else's but had I failed, he still would have been proud of me.

Like Jackie Robinson, he was a guy who would steal home. He liked surprises, upsets, come backs, and to do the unexpected. It made life more exciting for him and these attributes have rubbed off on me – no they are more than that. They are deeply imbedded in me and I thank him every day for being the extraordinary person that he was.

He was only 5'8" but he would take on anyone no matter how big they were. That's what he did when he took on AT&T and became President of the Local of the Communication Workers of America (CWA). He was intuitively very smart and courageous. He feared no one or anything. He would pick his spot and go for it.

Some of us lose control of our emotions to the point where we are dysfunctional. Luckily this never happened to me. But as we grow older and strive for our independence as young adults, our break from the womb is gradual until our first or second love affairs cause us to emotionally crash and burn. This happened to me at least twice where I was rejected by lovers whom I thought I would marry and therefore have a permanent attachment, a nexus or connection to a new foundation. When those relationships came to an end, I was devastated, overwhelmed with sadness and grief. Fortunately, I did not become psychotic but did suffer a deep sense of alienation that may have been exacerbated by my subconscious awareness that I was adopted.

This may seem like a giant reach for those who are not adopted, but once you learn that you are, there is a mindset of nearly infinite possibilities as to why we acted in certain ways. Were we motivated by genes, or life experience or pure independent thoughts? Life experience is the one given in that equation. Untraceable genes complicate the assessment of whether thoughts are original. Is a creative thought by a child original if in the body of a parent whose identity is not known?

While my adoptive father was a strong person, I have always identified with older male figures, not in a sexual way, but usually with great respect for their knowledge, life experience and leadership qualities. Was I subconsciously in search of a true father figure? Is that a natural tendency for males at any age because I still have awesome respect for older, male figures especially those with extreme life experiences? Was I satisfied with my adoptive father as a role model or was I in search of better one?

In The New York Times Magazine, an article by Lauren Slater entitled: *Is the World Ready for Medical Hallucinogens?* April 22, 2012, at 56, the author addresses the anxiety and depression experienced by those diagnosed with terminal illness. Having my two adoptive parents wither and die was hard enough but learning that I was adopted added to my unsettled feeling, one where I felt my entire foundation being taken away from me with nothing left to stand on except what I have made for myself. The search for roots may also lead to a search of inner self. For the first time in my life I felt not so much humbled, as weakened, and aged. My optimism about life was vanishing and so was my excitement for it. Instead of creating and planning my future, I felt more accepting of my own fate. I had lost some of my competitive zeal. I felt less self-determinative and more guarded or even overwhelmed by the forces of nature.

Learning that my biological parents were also dead, put a wall of death around me. My search would take me to their graves, to their spirits, if they existed. My search caused me to face my own mortality to the extent of having to check myself to make sure that I was not leaving this reality and becoming psychotic. I was thinking more existentially about life, meaning that I was posing questions to myself which were unanswerable or metaphysical. I was questioning not only life's meaning but my own existence. Rene Descartes proved his own existence or so be thought, by dismissing the question with his famous Latin phrase: "Cogito Ergo Sum" or "I think, therefore I am." I could see that the need to know or to be with the dead in some extraterrestrial space or afterlife, could cause a break with my own sanity just as it has with others.

The need to backtrack, to say things to those who are dead but that should have been said during their lifetimes, is there for most of us as part of the bereavement process. Some will quietly pray while others will speak aloud or hold séances in an effort to communicate with the dead. Some claim to have seen apparitions, or ghosts, or other phenomena. How much of this is real and how much are delusions, we will never know unless those who claim to see or hear these revelations in our presence where we can see or hear for ourselves provided, we too are not deluded. This brings us to the question of, what is our reality? Is it here with the living on the planet earth or is it more with the dead?

The Slater article refers to a number of controlled therapeutic studies where volunteers with terminal illnesses received dosages of psilocybin or other hallucinogenics. The results were remarkable and while not inducing faith *per se* did make the volunteers more mystical creating positive changes in attitude, mood and behavior with some stating: "Death is never just an ending but part of the process" and "My death does not end my personal existence." This higher consciousness level and the possibility of achieving it, is also cause for optimism that there may be reliable evidence of a hereafter. This is approaching faith, something my adoptive father always said "is the most important thing." On the other hand, when this world is caving in on you, why not look to the next even if it is just mystical and not real? Isn't this why Disney World and its films are so popular? This has been my dilemma in accepting faith even for its mystical value. The lost soul in me tells me to go there but the lawyer in me looks for the hard evidence. Being part of a flock has never appealed to me except that the energy created by the millions who do believe is impressive even though it is for the most part premised on blind faith without hard evidence to support it. Believing that God walked on the planet earth thousands of years ago lends itself to pure speculation rather than reliable science. Faith then is the antithesis of science, the enemy of it and vice versa.

These are some of the internal conflicts that adoptees face. The issues are subtle and therefore dangerous for both the knowing and the unknowing. Not knowing whether your biological parents gave you up for a better life or because of their indifference is a question too often not answered, thus creating currents of ripple, psychological affects for adoptees. Your search for the Karma of your biological parents too often comes up blank. This is why more adoptees favor full disclosure of DNA and biological facts about their natural parents but even more they want to know the rationale for their adoption and what their lives might have been like had they not been adopted. It is more than curiosity. It is a search for identity, for self. The unsettling fact of learning that you are adopted creates uncertainty in other aspects of your life.

The search inevitably leads to mixed feelings that are both positive and negative. In my case I have chosen to focus on the uplifting parts of adoption and the devotion or love given by adoptive parents to those whom they adopt as positive. But I am also certain that many adoptive children instead concentrate on the negative synergy of their adoption, the natural parents' abandonment of them and the insufficient nurturing that they received from their adoptive parents. In my case I have chosen to honor both my adoptive parents and at least my natural mother for possibly recognizing that a better life awaited me elsewhere. Her courageous decision not to abort me tells me a lot about her character just as if she had decided to abort me would, except I would not be here to feel one way or the other.

You learn as you go forward that you are not alone in making your search; in being adopted or in having feelings that run the gamut of good, bad and indifferent about yourself, other adoptees, your natural parents and even your selfless adoptive parents. Jeremy Harding, a contributing editor at the London Review of Books in his brilliantly written book" *Mother Country, Memoir of An Adopted Boy*, (Verso, 2010 at viii and ix) in a compelling account of his own adoption search and life states:

> *"I've tried to tell a story: this is not a campaigning book. Nevertheless, it's a powerful illustration of what can happen when an adopted person, whose birth certificate shows only the names of the adoptive parents, exercises a legal right to see the original birth certificate — a right extended to every adoptee in England and Wales but denied to their US counterparts in all but a handful of states. I've alluded to the laws in Britain in this book, but with the persistence of sealed adoption records in the US, where there may be as many as six million adoptees, I'm inclined to say something about the politics of secrecy."*

> *"Adoption has preoccupied state lawmakers since the middle of the nineteenth century. In 1851, when the Massachusetts state legislature deliberated what was best for children whose parents wouldn't or couldn't keep them, adoption and fostering were rough and ready processes. In 1854, the New York Children's Aid Society began ferrying poor children west from New York on 'orphan trains': interested takers would make their way to rail stations where they could see the arrivals on show and offer them placements. Many were put to work on farms in the Midwest. The orphan trains ran until the end of the 1920s, taking a quarter of a million young people out of big eastern cities. In that period, agencies and intermediaries*

sprang up to refine the process of 'matching' and a new category of professional care worker appeared".

In his book *Steve Jobs* by Walter Isaacson (Simon & Schuster, 2011) the author makes a point about Jobs' adoption:

> *"Greg Calhoun, who became close to Jobs right after college, saw another effect. 'Steve talked to me a lot about being abandoned and the pain that it caused,' he said. 'It made him independent. He followed the beat of a different drummer and that came from being in a different world than he was born into.'" at 5.*

As the Spring of 2012 approached, I was in search of my roots not for curiosity but for health reasons. Knowledge of my parent's health status or their DNA might enable me to avoid my own early demise. Similarly, my children and their children might benefit from such discoveries. I did not expect to learn that I am the rightful heir to a throne. I was also in search of the rationale for my rejection.

I discovered Anne C. Ferguson's (who supposed to be Anne S. Ferguson's daughter) home in Staten Island, first trying to communicate by letter and then phone calls. A lawyer intervened. The lawyer said she worked with Anne and offered to help her through what was a shock to her system. According to the lawyer she did not know anything about it but since she had another brother born in September 1946, she wondered whether Anne S. could have conceived that soon after and allow for my birth on May 29th, eight and a half or nine months later. I conferred with Doctor friends who told me that it was possible.

Anne C. decided that she would agree to meet and provide information if a DNA test showed our relationship as half-brother and half-sister. In spring 2012, I set up the DNA tests and paid for them. I never saw Anne C. or spoke to her. All dealings were through her attorney. In July 2012, the mitochondrial DNA results came back negative. We did not share a common biological mother. Therefore, if Anne S. was her mother, she could not be mine. If we did not have the same biological mother then why did Anne S. lie in adoption papers, by stating that she had me out of wedlock?

If a half-brother is available then we could rule in or out whether we share the same biological father. Harold died at the age of 60 in 1967. Was Anne S. covering up for a member of her own family, even Harold? Could I have been Harold's child out of wedlock or even a product of incest? Was Domestic Violence or abuse in this picture? Was Anne covering for a friend or relative? Was my adoptive father my real father concealing his own out-of-wedlock liaison? I will most likely never know the answers to these and other questions? Our primitive laws do not allow for discovery of these facts – they should – but until they do, I and countless others will be the victims of Secret Adoptions.

I am torn between feelings of admiration for Anne S. in apparently making a sacrifice for someone, to conceal their embarrassment and responsibility while I also have a frustration or even anger at the fact that lies permeated my adoption and that correct information is not available. Of course, my adoptive parents probably believed at the time that this was a benefit to them and to me in that I would not be spending my life in search of my biological parents, trying to reconnect with them as well as brothers and sisters. There is a comfort level in not knowing after you have made every effort to find out. In my case, I will be spending my time not in trying to resurrect the past with all the inhibitions, shackles and chains that go with it. Instead, each day I am discovering my own identity by paying more attention to my own best instincts and following them. As I build my life it is on a foundation of love, leadership and courage that my adoptive parents showed in taking me on with selfless devotion. That is what all adoptees should focus upon, not the vagaries or even negativity associated with being given up in the first place. After all, we should be thankful for being born and being given a better life than we might otherwise have had. Now we are in a position to better the lives of others. How lucky I am to have just been born and adopted by such good people.

Chapter V

Discovery

MIRACLES CAN HAPPEN, I suppose. This was better than winning the lottery. My youngest daughter, Francesca Eileen, in March of 2017, submitted her DNA to Ancestry.com. When she received the results back, she called me. "Dad, you were right!" I had never been right before; so, I said: "What do you mean?" She replied: "Well, you remember you said that you might be British, well my results came back, and I am thirty to sixty percent British so, you must be ninety percent British. I am getting you a test kit for your birthday."

So, I got the kit and submitted the DNA. It came back with an astounding result that I am 54% Irish, 34% Western European, and only 3% Italian. This is a bit of a shock since I have been a member of Tiro A Segno, the oldest ethnic club in the United States located on MacDougal Street in Manhattan's Greenwich Village and I have been a Past President of the Columbian Lawyers' Association and counsel to a number of Italian organizations. Revised test results later showed that I am 68 % Irish, 32 % British and 0% Italian.

The story does not end there. An Ancestry website provides you with an alleged family tree information, where you can find your never known relatives. Believe it or not, I got an email from Mary Sirchia, wherein she stated that she was related to me. In the beginning, I was questioning her information and was puzzled by it. So, I proceeded to send her an email and asked if she would read my book, *The Secret Adoption* (iUniverse 2011). Mary read the book and reported back to me that we are indeed related. She said that she knew who my biological mother was, and she informed me that I have a first cousin, Eileen King, who lives in Long Island. Also, I learned that Eileen's mother was my biological mother's sister, and she used to care for my mother until she was gone.

This information is then circulated among family members and I was reunited with them on November 4, 2017, in Danbury, Connecticut.

Some members of my new family feel that John Smith was not my father. Anne and John were estranged. It may be that Anne was trying to cover up her promiscuity or just wanted me to have a name – Donald Smith. After meeting my new family, all super, wonderful people, the weakest part of the clan appears to have been my mother and father. My first cousin, Eileen King and her late husband, cared for my aunt and my mother. My mother lived for a while with Eileen and my aunt. Eileen bought her a condominium in Strasburg, Pennsylvania. Anne went there to be with my older brother, John, who had opened a bar which later failed. John, my brother was born on February 1, 1939, in Brooklyn, New York. His full legal name was John Richard Smith. He apparently died of alcoholism. His daughter Christine, is wonderful and lives not far from me in Wantagh, Long Island. Her daughter Ashley has completed a second Master's Degree at Hofstra University and her son Christopher is a police officer in the N.Y.P.D.

The rumor in the family is that Anne must have been someone's mistress. When she died, she had a Will but had rarely, if ever, worked. She gave $600,000 to a church which she never attended. She just picked it out of the yellow pages. As far as I know, she made no effort during her lifetime to reach out to me or to advise family members of what happened to me, the lost baby of the family.

Everyone's life is easier as a WASP. My father, John, may have been a WASP but not a wealthy or privileged one. My life with the two of them would have been an unmitigated disaster. My adoptive parents were loving people. Growing up there was more emphasis placed on the Italian part of their background, I think because of the discrimination against Italians in the last century. The Irish had migrated here first following the potato famine in that country. Although the Irish were also discriminated against with signs reading: "The Irish Need Not Apply," they gradually made their way into Tammany Hall and the municipal unions where they dominated the police and fire departments.

The Italians began their migration fifty years later but they did not speak the language, there were quotas as to how many were allowed to come here and they were closed out of the municipal unions. This rampant discrimination forced them into the trades, the construction industry and even organized crime.

My adoptive mother, Eileen, was raised by a father, Francis, who was born in Glasgow, Scotland. Her mother was born here but her family came from Dublin, Ireland. Eileen was ostracized by her own family because she married an Italian, Louis. Louis was protective of her heritage while she was even more protective of his.

I grew up with a sense that the Italians were underdogs, having to fight against discrimination which had excluded them from business, the professions, politics, and better schools. Louis was a fighter, a smart and liberal thinker who identified with minorities. He played the violin, enjoyed singing songs from the opera, and excelled in boxing, baseball, and other sports. Excluded from traditional occupations, minorities such as the Italians gravitated toward sports and entertainment where they might make their way. Frank Sinatra and Joe DiMaggio were the shining examples of this. The emphasis in our home was more on sports than academics. This is one aspect of my upbringing which I regret. Having siblings might have produced more rivalry and a broader world view.

Louis became President of the Little League and Boy Scouts. He had his friends in the African American community and in the Jewish community who were also fighting against discrimination but making their way in business by outsmarting the WASPS who were trying to keep them down. It is no doubt that their influences played a role in my becoming a civil rights lawyer, still fighting for the underdogs and working just outside the system itself. The privileged still find their ways to keep us down – the poor, the middle class, the minorities, women, and people from the Blue States. I was raised as a proud New Yorker embraced by my fellow minorities. If I am a part WASP, it is too late for me to consider becoming part of that world. I will continue to enjoy my new family but will always be devoted to the minorities that have been and continue to be such an important part of my life.

The Black Lives Matter Movement of 2020 is bringing a long-overdue reckoning. With COVID-19 and a failing economy, this created a Perfect Storm that allowed the Movement to get traction. The Movement is creating change more significant than the Civil Rights Movement of 60 years ago. The difference now is the great masses of people throughout the world who are organized against the opposition that began 400 years ago when the first slave ship landed here in 1619. But more importantly, the multi-trillion-dollar bailouts for businesses and the stimulus packages have created the idea that police forces should be defunded and reorganized and that reparations may be possible. Confederate monuments are being taken down and politicians even in the Red States are beginning to realize that their time is past.

Chapter VI

Who Am I?

MY WIFE IS a great believer in "less is more", whereas I am a believer in more is just more. We all have attention deficit disorders to a degree for any subjects other than ourselves and members of our immediate family although in many cases attention does not transcend that far. So why bother writing if less is more? Why not just send out the usual Christmas photo and be done with it? The answers to these questions are both simple and profound, at least for me, since like most humans I am a bit of both, not having much time to contemplate the complex and reducing all to the simplest analysis. If our views of the world are products of our defense mechanisms or survival instincts – being happy is better than being sad. Being occasionally existential is not tolerated in a computer age where fact checking has taken the place of original thoughts. If introspection is to be replaced by iPhones, then I prefer to remain a dinosaur. If speech or conversation is to be replaced by text messages of one hundred twenty abbreviated characters or less, then I think it is past time to hit the pause button in this Orwellian/Kubrick Space Odyssey.

A lawyer I know, passes me in the courthouse and always greets me with the same greeting which is: "Are you living the dream?" I nod and mumble because my dream is not his. It is not a case of one size fits all. There is not one universal dream. I suspect that his dream has to do with fame and fortune. Even if the shallowness of my existence is to be measured by wealth which it will not be, I would never choose to be boastful about it.

In the latter stages of his life, Ezra Pound seemed to believe that there was a message in his silence, or he ran out of words, or the will to write them. In the law, silence may be viewed as acceptance. I have been a Judge in the Village of Westbury, Long Island for more than 29 years. Behind my Bench, there is a framed copy of the Declaration of Independence reminding me, if not everyone in my courtroom, that it is our duty to rebel against tyrannies and oppression. The oppressors are often those who prefer lockstep thinking, a uniform thought process. Every July 4th I hear and see fireworks going off all around me but few people realize what they are celebrating which is the start of an American revolution brought about by England's tyranny against us. While the Declaration was signed by slave owners, today's revolution except for that is not unlike what the Declaration stood for in 1776.

Cultivating my own independence or original thinking is essential for what I do as a lawyer. Finding solutions to complex problems requires free thinking, sometimes far outside the box of the status quo. In Candide, Voltaire wrote that: "we must cultivate our gardens." Writing is my way of cultivating my garden. Although, I shamefully confess to shelving at least one book by James Joyce, which I found to be unreadable I have additionally shelved others including an American author, Ernest Hemingway, which continue to collect dust for the same reason. I felt quite at home while visiting the Poets' Corner. I was standing next to Rudyard Kipling's grave when I saw, across from the site, Geoffrey Chaucer's stone casket. My aversion to the old or middle English language prompted me to recall the anonymous author and Anglo-Saxon poet, referred to by scholars as the "Beowulf". I was pleased to learn that my own grammatical faults would be forgiven by the Barristers Chambers at the Inns of Court where grammatical marks are not utilized at all in the streams of conscience that they call their legal briefs or at least a draft of them. I felt comfortable at Old Bailey among the scoundrels, both barristers and defendants, who inhabit that courthouse.

I write to bring my new family up to date on a few of my adventures. I write to clarify who this stranger is in their midst? While absent from the family for 71 years, they deserve to know more about this newest member of their family.

Chapter VII

The Trip of a Lifetime

THE TRIP OF a lifetime began as a birthday surprise for my wife, Wendy's, fiftieth birthday. The surprise was a trip on the Queen Mary II in its maiden voyage year. During the trip out of Manhattan to the Caribbean we had dinner with the Captain followed by a trip to the bridge where Wendy had the opportunity to steer the great ship. After learning of my adoption it was possibly a search for my English identity that caused me to enjoy that trip. The formality, cleanliness, luxury and elegance truly appealed to me but then again, it is hard to believe it would not appeal to everyone.

In Italy we stayed at the home of Cardinal Villa D'este on Lake Como, playing on the same tennis courts near the Swiss border that the Pope had played on a week earlier. I saw the last supper, attended the Opera at La Scala, and ate dinner at Caruso's table, eating his favorite meal of Ossobuco. I drove the Amalfi coast, stopping at cities and towns along the way. Siena, Orvieto, Rome, Venice (the home of 400 bridges) where we had lunch at the Hotel Cipriani. My wife, with her degree with Honors in Fine Arts from Duke University and Master's in Fine Arts from Pratt Institute led us to Padua, a small university town with a chapel hidden in its outskirts, where she located prized frescoes by Giotto. Thereafter we continued our trek to San Pietro at Positano, a hotel considered to be the finest in the world, but certainly in the Mediterranean. There in the hotel's log we read: "Living well is the best revenge."

The voyages in life have taken me to dinner at to the Queen's Table in Sam Lord's Castle in Barbados, where we dined with renowned attorney Milton Gould and his wife. Milton was the second part of Shea (as in Shea Stadium) Gould in New York. Milton had no fear. At another Federal Bar Council trip in Saint John's in the Virgin Islands, I had lunch with the late Supreme Court Justice, Thurgood Marshall. At about the same time, I met Marshall's great friend in the Court, William Brennan. In the meeting, with Justice Marshall I mentioned to him that Wendy and I had met Dr. Kenneth Clark at a housing conference in Philadelphia. Clark, famed psychologist from the City University of New York did the doll study of white and black dolls which was incorporated into what became known as the first Brandeis brief, enabling Marshall to win the case of *Brown v. the Board of Education* in 1954. That case, of course, overruled the Separate but Equal Doctrine of *Plessy vs. Ferguson* of 1896.

Politics was a part of my life. My adoptive father's father had been a District Leader in Tammany Hall. My adoptive father, Louis, was the President of the Communication Workers of America (C.W.A.), the Office Workers Local in Manhattan. The C.W.A. was known for being among the most liberal unions in the country. He became friendly with Alex Rose, the head of the Ladies Garment Workers Union and Senator Robert Wagner, Sr., both liberal icons.

I was brought up as a liberal Democrat, joining the New Democratic Coalition (N.D.C.), the left wing of the Party and becoming a Zone Leader. After Law School, I ran for election as a Democratic/Independent candidate for Supervisor in the Town of North Hempstead. I was endorsed by former Congressman, later Ambassador, Allard Lowenstein (dec.). Allard started the Dump Johnson Movement; had been the President of the National Students' Association (N.S.A.) and encouraged Bobby Kennedy to run for the Presidency in 1968. I was also endorsed by Tom Downey, the youngest Congressman ever elected at age twenty-five; Congressman Peter Rodino, the Head of the Watergate Impeachment Committee and Ted Kennedy. I lost the election. The Town had been controlled by Republicans for seventy – five years.

The Democrats were holding a midterm National Convention in 1978. I was elected as Nassau Delegate. In my County the Republicans controlled everything. I was interested in public service but could not seem to break into it as a Democrat, so in 1978 I switched my registration to Republican. My candidate for the Assembly lost by 29 votes, and everyone thought that I would be the next Republican candidate for the Assembly in 1980. That did not happen, but I was asked to head up the National Nationalities Committee of Ronald Reagan in 1980 which I did. I also became a member of the Republican Party Chairman's Club, comprised of the so – called "Fat Cats" in the Party of which I was not one. But at the time I was representing Anthony Casamento, a World War II hero who had been denied the Congressional Medal of Honor by four Presidents. I persuaded Governor Reagan to come to New York to announce that if elected President, he would give the Congressional Medal of Honor to Casamento. This strategy was geared to getting the votes of veterans and Italian Americans. The Democrats learned of my efforts and in September 1980. President Carter gave the Congressional Medal of Honor to Casamento. Reagan won anyway and with the Italian votes.

Wendy and I attended the Inauguration and the New York State Ball in Washington, D.C. We met Nancy and President Reagan. I was offered a position in the Department of Justice in the Civil Rights Division, which I could not take because I already had a private practice growing back in New York. Wendy and I bought our house in 1980, the one in which we still live.

After law school, I was offered a job as counsel at the New York State Grievance Committee and another with a government agency in Washington D.C. which I also did not take. My life's path really started changing for me in 1979-1980, switching from a primary interest in politics to being an attorney and trial lawyer. I came to view trial lawyers as honorable people. Some politicians take aim at them without understanding that they are the true champions of liberty, freedom and our Constitution. What I learned about politics is the same as what I learned when I left sports. To get it out of your system, you have to go "cold turkey".

Chapter VIII

Early Life

MY EARLY LIFE was all about sports. School work was not of interest to me. Basketball and baseball were my primary activities. I liked the fact that older boys admired my ability to break through them on the asphalt basketball court. I can remember staying at that court for hours on cold winter days, all by myself just practicing my shots. My adoptive father Louis, had been a semi-pro, sandlot baseball player. He took me back to the Brooklyn Dodgers locker room, where I met Emmett Kelly – the clown; Gil Hodges; Pee Wee Reese; Roy Campanella and Duke Snider. Louis became the President of the Central Nassau Athletic Association and Chairman of the Boy Scouts local troop 469. He was a great organizer and built up the fledging little league to a Pony League, Babe Ruth and Connie Mack Leagues. He also ran a winter basketball program. It was all good. I made it to the Pony League All-Stars. I was a pitcher and Louis taught me how to pitch; curveballs, side arms, submarines, knuckleballs, and changeups.

I attended Bowling Green Elementary School in East Meadow from kindergarten through fifth grade. I then attended Sacred Heart Seminary, a co-ed day school in Hempstead run by the nuns of Saint Joseph, where their reputation is similar to that of the Jesuits; very smart and very tough. My parents and the nuns taught me how to be a gentleman. I had to wear a tie and uniform every day. I had my own charge card at Browning King 5th Avenue, where I was always greeted as "Master Tom." Except during the summer, I was no longer involved in sports. I became a leader in the school which stood adjacent to

Sacred Heart Academy, the leading Catholic all girls high school in Nassau County. My adoptive mother Eileen, was the President of the Parents' Association and ran fashion shows and other fundraisers for the school. She had been a model in the 1930s and 1940s. She always wore magnificent, classy hats. She was a beauty beyond compare. Everyone admired her good looks but she was very humble about that. Until I learned of my adoption, I thought that I had inherited some of that.

Our home in East Meadow was right around the corner from the Carmen Avenue Pool. When Bill Levitt built Levittown after WWII, he also built schools, shopping centers, and nine public, outdoor swimming pools. The Carmen Avenue Pool was where I learned how to swim. When Eileen was growing up, her parents had a home in the Rockaways, where she learned how to swim. She taught me how to swim and how to read.

When I was around nine and ten, my mother would pick me up after school and drive me to Brooklyn Technical High School, where I swam twice a week during the winter. I was a member of the Knickerbocker Swim Club and competed in races throughout New York City. While we were middle class, my mother and father treated me to a somewhat privileged upbringing, sometimes making me feel like royalty, separate and apart from other young people with whom I grew up. They were always striving to give me the best of what they could. I always had the best sports equipment, my own room, a television. I even had a motorized go-cart. My room was pine paneled by my father, it had a built-in desk and bookshelves. They never followed the crowd. Neither did I. This is what started my independent way of thinking and living. It has survived within me to this day.

After I graduated from Sacred Heart Seminary at the end of the eighth grade, both my parents became swim coaches at the Carmen Avenue Pool. It was there we won the Levittown Swimming Championship at the end of the summer. After winning two events and it became clear that I might have some ability in competitive swimming. We were not aware of it at the time but I also had atrial fibrillation, an irregular heartbeat, which reduces your efficiency up to twenty-five percent.

My ingenious father found a way to have me attend the Westbury Junior High School, in a district where we did not live. The high school there had an indoor swimming pool, which East Meadow School District did not have. I tried out for the Junior High School football team, whose coach took a liking to me. I played defensive end and linebacker. After the football season, I joined the high school swimming team, not making it to the finals in the County Swim Championship in my event of the 400-yard freestyle but promising myself to return the following year and win. After my freshman year, my parents enrolled me in an Olympic Development training program at the Renaissance Country Club in Roslyn. It was organized by Bob Burke, whose daughter Lynn from the Flushing YMCA had gone to Santa Clara, California to train and won two gold medals in the 1960 Rome Olympics. Mr. Burke had recruited Dick Krempecki, the coach of Saint John's University to be our coach. The program was modeled after the famed Santa Clara Swim Club's Program of two long course workouts per day. Renaissance had a fifty-meter pool. It was 1962 and the first time that I had really trained. It was my break through summer. One of our swimmers, Billy Shrout, made it to the finals of the outdoor senior national Amateur Athletic Union Championships that year in the 200 meters freestyle. We watched him on ABC television's Wide World of Sports with Jim Mackay.

Now in tenth grade at Westbury High School the coaching was deficient. Instead of training with the high school team, my father and mother once again found a better place for me. They got me to train at Adelphi University under an NCAA Small College All – American, Vinny Santos, who also taught in the Westbury Junior High School. I won the County Swim Championship in the 400-yard freestyle and competed in the State Public High School Championships where I placed fifth.

Plainview Old Bethpage High School was a Mecca of competitive swimming in the northeast. Its coach, Charles Schlegel, was hardcore. The Renaissance program had ended and even though I was from a rival school, I decided to train that summer, 1963, with Coach Schlegel at the Woodbury Country Club. By now I had learned that hard work can lead to success. I also learned that I could work harder than anyone else.

That summer I began to coach myself in addition to what coach Schlegel provided. My thinking was that if I wanted to be the best, I had to work harder than everyone else. Since Schlegel's swimmers were the best, I had to work harder than them.

My father would drive me to Woodbury Country Club, where I would literally break in, chasing the ducks out of the pool and started to swim by 5:30 a.m. The pool was not heated. The water was cold. I invented a gallon can to drag behind me, creating resistance and I used hand paddles for the same reason. My workout would end at 7 a.m. when I would then workout for two hours with coach Schlegel from 7 a.m. to 9 a.m. in an unlined fifty-yard pool (Olympic size pools have lane lines painted on the bottom and are fifty meters in length, a meter being equal to 39 inches). I had a free membership at Woodbury in return for acting as a lifeguard but at 11:30 a.m. we would be picked up by our parents and driven to Plainview Old Bethpage High School, where we would workout for one and a half hours. It was just Fred Schneider and myself. His mother and mine would alternate taking us to and from the high school and return us to the country club thereafter where in the afternoon I would lifeguard at Woodbury which paid for my use of the pool and membership. I did not receive a salary. From 5:30 – 7:30 p.m. we would again workout at Woodbury with Coach Schlegel. Once home and after having a steak dinner I would run a mile, lift weights and go to sleep. This was my exhausting schedule day in and day out.

Coach Schlegel was a winner. He was a great leader, inspiring excellence, and success. That summer I decided to switch schools in order to attend Plainview. This caused a big investigation, by the New York State Public High School Athletic Association over Coach Schlegel's alleged recruiting practices. My mother drove me each day to and from Plainview. By then my parents had moved to Westbury thinking that I would have a legal residence in that District, where I had won the County championship.

Charlie had early morning workouts 6-8 a.m., starting in September. I would then sneak in for workouts during study halls, lunch hours and after school. At the end of my junior year I won the County and State Championships and set a State record in the

400-yard freestyle. I also placed second in the Eastern Interscholastic Championships. Completing my junior year in Plainview, next came the summer of 1964. The Olympic Games were to be held later that year in Tokyo.

I started the summer swimming with Charlie again, but he was not focused on the Olympic Games. My father made arrangements for me to train at the North Jersey Swimming Association. Robert Alexander, a/k/a/ Mr. "A", who had been the coach at the Knickerbocker Swim Club in Brooklyn when I swam there, owned a training camp in a lake in Wayne, New Jersey. I did not realize it at that time, but it was really a camp for sprinters of which I was not one. But it was filled with amazing east coast talents, all geared to making the Olympic Team. There was Dick McDonough from Villanova, who had won the Pan American Games the year before beating Don Schollander, who in 1964 won four Gold Medals in the Olympics. There was also Bill Shrout, who was leaving Brooklyn Tech for Harvard; Rick Girdler, also of Villanova who set a world record in 1965; Jack Geoghegan, an All-American from Villanova; Bill Steuk, an All American from Colgate; two world class backstrokers, Thompson Mann from the University of North Carolina and Jed Graef from Princeton. Patience Sherman was the best of the females.

My father made arrangements for me to live in North Jersey by running an ad in a church bulletin. Sure enough, I wound up living with the Demorests for two summers and then lived in Franklin Lakes at the home of the Chairman of the Board of American Cyanamid Corporation, Ralph Roland. His children also swam with Mr. "A" and I would drive them to and from workouts each day in the family Mustang convertible. In my final year there, in 1967, I commuted from New York each day.

In 1964, Thompson, Jed, and Patience made the Olympic Team. Thompson and Jed, each set world records in Tokyo, winning individual gold medals. Patience won a gold medal on a world record relay team.

In September 1964 I returned to Plainview for my senior year. I had a girlfriend from the previous year, Linda, and although we never exchanged rings as was the custom back then, we were for all intents and purposes "going steady". She was my first girlfriend and my parents also took a liking to her. She was one of four girls, the second oldest and her father Lewis took a liking to me. Linda and I were together for three and a half years and breaking up, was very hard on me. Being rejected is always hard on the human spirit. I cried.

Chapter IX

Swimming Past

IN MY SENIOR year I set state records in the 400-yard freestyle; 200-yard freestyle; 100-yard backstroke and 200-yard individual medley. I won the 400 yard and 200yard freestyle events in the Eastern Interscholastic Championships. I won the medley and 400-yard freestyle events in the County and State Championships. I had also been on Plainview's 200-yard freestyle relay, replaced by Mike Sinkinson, my best friend at Plainview, who went on to become an NCAA All – American at Bucknell. That high school relay team also won All – American Honors. I was honored to receive both the County and High School Outstanding Swimmer Awards.

From 1964-1967 I had also won the two events each year in Regional Championships (later known, as the Empire Games) usually held in Saratoga, New York. By 1965 I was recruited by every major swimming powerhouse in the nation. In retrospect, I made the mistake of not going to California to train and attend school there beginning in 1965 or even 1964. Instead, I wound up winning a full scholarship at Ohio State University. It had won more NCAA Championships than any other school in the nation. It won its last championship in 1963. It had produced countless Olympians and world record holders. When I attended school there, one of my teammates was Mike Finneran, who later scored perfect 10s in the three-meter diving competition in the Mexico City Olympics. The diving Coach was Ron O'Brien, who later went on to became the Olympic Coach, bringing Greg Louganis, among many others, to fame and fortune.

Coach Schlegel had attended Ohio State and that may have had something to do with my selection and me receiving a full scholarship. I was really gung - ho on Ohio State, but probably too immature to adapt. I was terribly homesick for my parents and Linda. I was running up phone bills of over $200.00 dollars per month, writing letters home almost every day. In my first year at Ohio State, I hardly got by academically and really did not improve my times. Freshmen were not permitted to compete in varsity competitions. I did not feel, that I was measuring up to Big Ten standards. I had pledged a national fraternity, Beta Theta Pi, the most popular frat house on campus but I could not adapt or accept their initiation rites of passage to full membership. My dream of Olympic gold seemed to be fading. I was accustomed to being the best or at least believing that I might become the best. But none of that was clicking. As a New Yorker in a school of 50,000 students where football was really its most celebrated sport, I felt alone. As one of five so called "professional sports" at Ohio State, the swimming team received eight full scholarships per year whereas the football team received twenty-eight. Everything at O.S.U. centered around the football team and its demanding coach, Woody Hayes.

I returned to Ohio State for my sophomore year, still feeling homesick and not really achieving. That December I decided to attend the College Swim Forum in Fort Lauderdale to train. I went on my own. When I came back to New York I got the news that my grade point had dipped, where I would be ineligible. So, I was now in a limbo, thinking that my swimming career was over, figuring that I was most likely headed to Vietnam. But then again, Louis came to the rescue. He was just a miracle worker. He had fond memories of Adelphi and may have imagined that I might still come back as a baseball player. He arranged for me to be interviewed by the Dean of Admissions, Dan Bratton.

My relationship with Linda was fading. After all, I was no longer a sport celebrity trying to break into the big time. I was heading toward a life in mediocrity. I had no choices at that point about where my life was headed. I was no longer in control of my own destiny. She still had options. So why not jump ship?

For anyone with big goals, aiming close and not getting there is a great disappointment and grounds for depression, especially if you have made a large effort in a commitment over time as I had. Competitive swimming was my life. I had started a swimming log in 1960's entering every workout, everyday together with my comments about performance. When I had finally finished competing in 1970 the log was 3000 pages. Most parents in raising their children do not have a clue about what is required for true excellence in sports especially if the children are not naturally gifted. The national and international competition requires a whole other level of commitment, far beyond what most parents and athletes envision. For example, I published my first article on backstroke techniques in an international sports publication when I was just seventeen. I published two more after that, one which revolutionized the starting systems for races so that the signal for the start of a race is heard at the same time by all competitors. It used to be that the starter's gun would be heard a tenth of a second later for swimmers in lane eight, a distance of at least twenty-one meters from the starter. My study had to do with the speed of sound. If the starter's flash of the gun was seen, then the speed of light which travels faster than the speed of a sound would give that competitor even more of an advantage. In some cases, people were not making the Olympic Team by one-tenth of a second. Under the old timing system before the advent of touchpads and computerized timing systems which go to thousands of a second, some were not making the Olympic Team by a tenth of a second, the time it took for the sound to travel from the starter to lane eight. There were three timers on a lane using Bulova stopwatches. In the 1964 Olympic Trials held in the Astoria Pool in New York City, my father was a timer at one of the center lanes with Mrs. Schollander, Don's mother. Don won four gold medals in the Tokyo Olympics.

Eileen prepared recorded times by all of my competitors from around the nation so that I could see how my rivals were progressing. I was both a subscriber to Swimming World and Swimming Technique Magazines. I could spout the times and history of every local, national and international competitor to the tenth of a second. The memorization of them became second nature to me. You had to know how everyone was training for better or worse, how they fared over time, when they hit their peaks and when they did not. This is how you measured your own potential against them. It was a constant study of strengths and weaknesses in human behavior. By plotting their times throughout the year and learning of their training methods you could more or less determine whether they would be peaked during championships, how much their times were likely to drop and whether you could prevail against them. Today this kind of data is used in all sports. Coaches no longer rely on just their instincts and life experience alone.

When I got to Adelphi, I felt like I was pretty well washed up as a serious athlete. As a transfer student, I would be ineligible for at least a year. At the start of 1967, I was an evening student, matriculating with twelve credits and staying out of the draft. When I arrived at Adelphi, I met some people who gradually restored some of my faith and confidence in myself. I could see that they at least had the potential for big time sporting achievements. At first, I met Bill Irwin, the swimming coach. He had been a sprinter at Rutgers University winning the fifty-yard freestyle in the Eastern Intercollegiate Championships in 1948. He had also been on a National Championship Relay Team. He had been the Chairman of New York Athletic Club Swimming Committee. He was a star in every sense of the word, a first-class gentleman who wore a tie and sports jacket every day. He knew his swimming and sports history, but he was more of a Renaissance man who knew a lot about everything. He enjoyed writing and had read Will Durant's History of Civilization twice. He had two sons who attended the Horace Mann, New York City's premier prep school. Each later graduated from Harvard. From the time I met him in 1967 until his death on October 30, 2017, he was my best friend. In 1977 he became the Best Man at my wedding.

Jim Bedell was the Athletic Director who also impressed me as a guy on his way to the big time. He had brought in other coaches who were capable of national prominence. You could see it and feel it. There was Menaheim Less, who had just earned his Ph.D. at Penn State in Physical Education and physiology. He knew body mechanics; the latest techniques and training methods in all sports. He became the soccer coach recruiting athletes from Israel and bringing to Adelphi an NCAA University Division Championship. So, did Paul Dougherty the lacrosse coach and Ron Bazil came to us from Jamaica High School. He recruited African American track stars including Bob Beamon who won a gold medal in 1968 in Mexico City Olympics, setting a world record in the broad jump. He also assembled a relay team that set a world record in the indoor mile. I continued to train, working out once a day. I could not compete in intercollegiate competition but I did compete in the Amateur Athletic Union Competition. My exit from Ohio State created quite a stir locally. My failure there made me feel embarrassed and humiliated.

Unbeknownst to me, I was undergoing a metamorphosis at Adelphi. I figured my swimming career was about over, so I began studying for the first time. The classes were smaller, the professors were reachable, whereas at Ohio State I had nine thousand fellow students in my freshman math, English and psychology classes. At Ohio State I had written just one letter to the campus newspaper, The Lantern. At Adelphi, I was taking an interest in learning and writing. My first article was a book review of William F. Buckley's first book: *Man and God at Yale.*

All of this and much more came out later. I was still finding my way as a fledgling college student. Gradually my grades were coming up. I attended summer school, also at night, commuting to and from New Jersey each day. My parents were my benefactors. I did not have a job, I was a drain on them, but they had faith and love.

I started writing for the school newspaper, the Delphian. I ran for and became President of the Men's Athletic Association. It was my first elective office. I was still swimming once a day, just working out. Irwin was letting me train. It was my life's blood. Like my parents, Irwin had the same faith in me. I attended Adelphi's meets as a spectator. The team was lack luster, unlike Plainview or Ohio State. I was still competing in AAU competition.

I began attending school events. Dan Bratton, the Dean of Admissions told me to get involved and I did. It was the 1960s. College campuses across the country were alive with debates and protests against the Vietnam War. I was making a transformation from being solely involved in sports to seeing a world outside of sports.

At the end of the 1968 season, I still had not competed in a college meet. It was now three years since I completed a high school. Adelphi chose to send me to the National Association of Intercollegiate Athletics

Association Championships in Minnesota, a/k/a/ the NAIAs. I won the 200-yard freestyle, taking seconds in the 500 yard and 1650-yard freestyle events but my eligibility was challenged and Jim Bedell, our Athletic Director, had to fly out to Minnesota with my records. I was determined to be eligible. Because of my win, I was automatically qualified for the United States Olympic Team trials which were held in Long Beach, California later that year.

That summer I trained with Irwin. Our workouts were held from 6 a.m. until 8 a.m. each day at the Manorhaven pool on the north shore. The water like most New York pools in that era before heaters, was very cold. An ideal water temperature for workouts is 76 degrees. The water temperature in Manorhaven was probably in the low 60s. This was another mistake by me in not going out to California for the second time, but Irwin was making such an effort, I felt like I had to stay in New York. After the Manorhaven workout, which was about thirty minutes from my home, I would go to North Hempstead Country Club, where Irwin was a Pool Director. I would swim there from 9 a.m. to 10:30 a.m. It was a workout in a short course pool of 25 yards. It was a make shift set up. I had no one to train with of my ability or better.

After Manorhaven and North Hempstead, Monday through Friday, I would travel to the Hamilton Fisch Pool in lower Manhattan to train with my friend Paul Katz. The workouts were run by his father Leon, a Physics Professor at one of the City Colleges. The pool was unlined, meaning that it had no racing lanes but it was long course and 50 meters. The pool was in a bad neighborhood. It was a City pool from the 1930s. It took me more than an hour to get there each day and the same amount of time on the way back.

Paul had attended Seward Park High School, also on the lower east side. He had managed to score perfect 800's on his math and English SAT's; he was heading to Yale in the Fall.

Since the pool was in the "hood", during the hot summers people from the neighborhood would break in at night. The pool was probably more populated at that time then it was during the day. The pool was closed to the public during lunch from 12 noon to 1:30 p.m. when we would workout. Sometimes there would be feces on the bottom, or lifeguard stands thrown into the pool from the previous night. During our workouts pimps and drug dealers would be outside of the fences, making fun of us.

At night I trained by myself in the Cantiague Park Pool from 5:30–7:30. I had to put up my own line during a public session. I had no coach. My father would come and hold the watch. The pool was not fast. The water was rough and young children would come into my lane. Nonetheless, from a push off in that pool, meaning not from a dive, I clocked my best time for 400 meters two weeks before the trials. I was under 4:20 and with tapering I figured I might be able to bring it down another five to ten seconds. I figured that around 4:12 would qualify for the final in the trials. Once in the top eight, anything can happen. I did not have that much speed but I could hold a pace. I was a "negative split" swimmer much like Roger Bannister in 1954 when he broke the 4-minute mile in track. His splits for each quarter were 1 minute until the final quarter at 59 seconds. I would always come back faster in the second part of the race. If I could go out in the first 200 meters at 2:06, I could probably get back in about the same time during the second part of the race of 200 meters.

There was a conversion table at the time where you could determine the meters to yards. At 400 meters the conversion time was 36 seconds. At 400 meters, if my time was 4:24 that would convert to 3:48 in yards. Meaning that I would have to swim at 1:54 for every 200 yards. This was about 17 seconds under my New York State High School record at 400 yards.

My best time in college for 200 yards freestyle was only 1:48.6. Replicating that twice could bring me out to about 3:37 in yards and probably around 4:12 for 400 meters. Thus, I could make the final.

The Olympic trials during the summer of 1968 were held in Long Beach, California. There was a new pool, it was shallow at one end, therefore making it a "slow pool" hydrodynamically. I was in the first heat of the first event, 200 meters freestyle. Next to me was Michael Burton, the unrivaled world record holder at 1500 meters at the time. I came in at 2:05 and he came in at just under two minutes.

Usually, we shaved our bodies for the meet; it gives you a tingling feeling when you hit the water. You are able to feel the water better; there is less friction. Paul managed to convince me to also shave my head, which I did. It turned out that there were only three shaved heads at the trials. There is a photo of me at the trials in *The Secret Adoption* (iUniverse, 2011) with my shaved head.

When we arrived in Long Beach, the scoreboards in the pool gave us an inspiring message: *"In Great Attempts It Is Glorious Even to Fail."* I have kept that as a lifelong personal motto by which I live my life. My clients have said: "Mr. Liotti, you've got the game," meaning I am willing to take a shot, take a gamble in fighting for an underdog who seemingly has a losing case. You've got to step up to the plate in order to upset the apple cart. There is nothing quite like winning against an arrogant, over confident foe.

I finished the trials at 400 meters in 14th place which meant that I was in about the same place in the world. The top two finishers in each event make the Olympic Team and the third-place finishers go as an alternate. Since the United States was dominant in world swimming, our athletes would traditionally win far more gold medals than any other nation.

After the trials Paul and I headed to Southern California and Tijuana, Mexico. It was my first time outside the country. We attended a bull fight and jai alai there. Tijuana is a border town, not far from the San Diego naval base and at the time, a den of iniquity.

Upon returning home I was back at Adelphi becoming more involved in student activities. My awareness of the world outside of sports was increasing. I was now competing in dual meets. I was undefeated. In 1969 I competed in the NCAA Small College Championships, placing second in two events and making All-American in three events. Student protests were happening everywhere. Bobby Kennedy and Martin Luther King, Jr. were both assassinated in 1968. While some of my fellow jocks were oblivious to the political turmoil, I was not. I organized the Metropolitan Association of Student Governments, a loosely organized group of student governments from colleges and universities in the Metropolitan area put together to lobby for social change. Several meetings were held which I chaired but a few obstructionists prevented it from really getting off the ground. It was generally to be a non-violent alternative to peace protests at Columbia University which were becoming more violent with students taking over buildings and forming sit – ins. The Students for a Democratic Society (SDS) also had a violent fringe group known as the Weathermen. I attended the National SDS Convention held at Harvard in 1970 and marched in protest against the ROTC at Boston University.

1970 was a volatile year at college campuses. Nixon was in the White House. Four students were shot and killed at Kent State by National Guardsmen, one of them Jeffrey Miller, had attended a neighboring high school in Plainview. I have dedicated a portion of my life to him although we never met. Other students at Jackson State in Mississippi were also killed. The war was raging in Vietnam. I was elected to be a commencement speaker. Another student speaker elected, was Rene Brown. As an African American woman, she had her own story to tell. Margaret Chase Smith, the Conservative Republican U.S. Senator from Maine, was also a featured speaker.

The President called a meeting in his office of all the speakers. He wanted to know what everyone planned to say. He was worried about a riot, walkout, a protest or whatever. He was just worried. He went around the table, everyone told him what they planned to say. Much to his dismay, sensing that this might be an attempt to censor me, I refused to say anything about my speech. When Commencement Day arrived, there were at least 10,000 people in the audience. The F.B. I. and local cops were all over me. I sat next to Senator Margaret Chase Smith. When it became my turn to speak, I had prepared a tape which was set to be played over the public address system. Deborah, my girlfriend at the time, my father and Irwin were all standing guard over it so that the F.B.I. and local cops could not interfere. For eight minutes it played sounds of the 1960's; music, speeches, and sound effects from the era such as bombs and gun fire. It boomed across the field. Some students and faculty gave it a standing ovation. Some exclaimed: "Far Out." I could hear President Vevier behind me saying that he was going to shut it down. I spoke for another ten minutes. Newsday carried my quote as a headline the next day: "For those too busy surviving, will they hear us?"

I decided that I wanted to be part of the solution to society's problems. I wanted to be a leader in politics like the Kennedys or Congressman Allard Lowenstein. I wanted to be like Ralph Nader who was then making his way as a consumer advocate. That summer I took two courses in the Adelphi graduate school of business in Macro and Micro Economics. In the Fall of 1970, I was employed as a health teacher in Great Neck North Junior High School. I was also the Head swimming coach at the United States Merchant Marine Academy. I decided that I needed to do more to prepare myself for public service, or to eventually become a lawyer. I enrolled in the evening Master of Public Administration program at the Bernard M. Baruch Graduate School of Business and Public Administration of the City University of New York at 23rd Street and Lexington Avenue in Manhattan. I was also accepted at N.Y.U. which had a 48-credit program whereas Baruch was a lot less money per credit and only 30 credits plus two 3 credit thesis courses. My Master's Thesis was entitled: *Ralph Nader's Impact on Governmental Action for Consumer Protection.* I left my Great Neck teaching position after six months. Pubescent seventh and eighth grade junior high school students and I did not get along. I then did substitute teaching; continued in my Master's Program and coaching. In the summer of 1970, I was the Pool and Beach Director at Sands Point Bath and Tennis Club where F. Scott Fitzgerald and John Philip Sousa had been members. I ran for election to the Westbury School Board. It was a six-candidate race, only three could be elected. I finished fourth, losing by just 40 votes.

My swimmers were doing really well. I produced five All – Americans in two years. The Merchant Marine Academy had never had All – Americans. I was voted as an Outstanding Coach at the Academy and in the Metropolitan area by my fellow swim coaches.

In 1969, I decided to take a stand in student politics. I ran for the Vice President of the Students' Association. I was elected. That summer I worked as a student intern in the Office of Admissions. There I met Deborah, an incoming student from Alexandria, Virginia. Adelphi had gotten a new President, Charles Vevier (dec.). He had been an administrator at Cornell. I did not like his grandiosity. He had an inauguration for himself which I called a coronation. That fall as I started my term, Al Fisher who had been elected President was called up to the National Guard. He left school. I then became the Co-President of the Students' Association with Cynthia Favata, who later became a lawyer and Federal District Court Judge in the Eastern District of Pennsylvania, Philadelphia.

I was a student activist proposing resolutions at every Student Council meeting which were always adopted. We had our own attorney. I was still completely unbeaten in dual meets, but not training in swimming as hard as I once did. Deborah and I were boyfriend and girlfriend. I still had a campus radio show and I was writing for the school newspaper. My father Louis became the President of the Parents' Association. He and an assistant Dean created an FM Radio station for Adelphi. In the Spring I competed once again in the NCAAs finishing second and making it to All – American status again in two events.

Chapter X

A Chance to Change the World

WHEN I WAS growing up, Louis was still playing softball. His will to win was extraordinary. He was a class act, but he could get down and dirty. He had been in the Golden Gloves so, as men sometimes say: "he could handle himself." In reality, he would "duke it out" with anyone. He was amazing. At five feet eight inches, he could take on anyone. He did not care. He feared no one. His respect meant everything to me because I thought so much of him.

He was such a fighter that I felt I could never measure up to him. He was smart as hell but knew how to go for the jugular. He was like Jackie Robinson, one of his heroes. He was the kind of guy who would not just steal second or third base. He would steal home. He always embraced the underdog because he viewed himself as one. He was a proud Italian American like all others. He was always discriminated against because of his ethnicity but never complained about it. The higher-ups in corporate management did not have to say it, but they discriminated.

When he played softball, it was with other semi-pro ballplayers. I watched him steal home with metal spikes up high. As a union organizer, he had a lawyer, Jules Buckbinder from Manhattan and Kings Point. Buckbinder did not have children. My father talked Buckbinder into taking me into the City with him to teach me the ropes of practicing law. My father always wanted to be a lawyer. When I was twelve and for about a year, my father would drive me to Buckbinder's home in Kings Point every Saturday morning. We would then be driven by

Buckbinder's chauffeur into the City and the Woolworth Building (at one time, the third-largest building in the world with a lobby that is renowned for its beauty) where Buckbinder had his office. The chauffeur was dressed in a gray uniform with black boots, epilates, and gold buttons. His boots were spit shinned. The Rolls Royce would pull up. The chauffeur would open the door and I would be out first, followed by Mr. Buckbinder, wearing a top hat, carrying a pearl-handled cane which he did not need, except for appearances. The pedestrians would stop because it was as if royalty was arriving. He wore vests as I now often do. I would sit next to him as he held court. Young Associate lawyers would come before him always wearing their ties and jackets with clients sometimes in tow. Buckbinder was like a God or icon. They would come before him waiting for his wise counsel: "yes sir, no sir" is what they would say. Buckbinder was a King. He was a general practitioner but he knew the City like no other. By 1 p.m. we would be driven for lunch at the Wall Street Club where the barons would gather and pay homage to him. Buckbinder was a Jewish lawyer, and therefore an outsider, but he had everyone's respect because he had made it. He was rich. He had powerful friends everywhere. He could get things done everywhere, at any time. I learned the business of law by watching the best. I saw how he carried himself. A man of the streets, who never forgot where he came from, which I believe were the tenements of the lower east side of New York, the housing for immigrants at the turn of the 20th Century. Buckbinder had risen to the top from one of the poorest neighborhoods of New York.

By August, 1972 I decided to leave coaching for law school. That summer I was helping Irwin to organize and train swimmers in an Olympic Development Program. Two Olympic coaches came to show their support. I took one swimmer to the Olympic Trials in Cincinnati that summer. Another of my swimmers won the National Junior Olympics in two events, beating a future medalist in the 1976 Olympics.

I really had no money. I was riding my bike two and from practices, or my great girlfriend, Debora Pitman would drive me. I was in flux, in disarray, but still had my goals in mind. I had choices – stay at the Academy; accept a coaching position to mentor the national swim team in Hong Kong or try to go to law school. But it was August and law schools were no longer accepting applications. My father, once again going into his bag of tricks, found the Delaware Law School in Wilmington, Delaware, which was founded as a private law school the year before in 1971 by Dean Alfred Avins (dec.). I applied and was accepted. The school was not yet approved for accreditation by the American Bar Association, which would be a prerequisite for taking the Bar examinations in most states.

If this was my only option, I had to give it a shot and take my chances. I enrolled as an evening student and I was a substitute, teaching in the ghetto schools of Wilmington during the day. I found a one-bedroom apartment. At first, I did not have a car, so I had to use a bike to get to and from the school. I turned down a coaching position in Wilmington. I joined the Wilmington YMCA and tried to workout every day. I had little money for food. Debora Pitman and I had broken up but my parents, as always, were supportive, helping me with tuition, books and other expenses. I was 25. I began to study very hard due to the amount of work that you must do just to keep up with your classmates but the law is not difficult to comprehend. Everything is very logical but you do read a lot. Since I was uncertain of my progress as a law student like most first years, I was paranoid and probably over studying but when the grades came out, I had done well, ranking pretty high in my class that first semester with essentially all B's. I felt confident. It looked like I would be able to do this. I was switching on and off between day an evening classes. Parents and students were very much involved in securing accreditation for the law school. The problem was that Dean Avins was such a conservative and his view of an independent, conservative law school did not coincide with the A.B.A.'s Accreditation Committee's views.

Avins was a genius. He had earned seven degrees by the time he was thirty-five; had published numerous law review articles, two books and argued several cases in the Supreme Court of the United States. His achievements were a shining light and very inspirational at least as far as I was concerned.

In 1971 he started the school by running classes in the YMCA. In the summer of 1972, he purchased the Penn Central Law Library or it was given to him and had students load tractor trailer trucks, also owned by students with 30,000 pounds of used law books which he then sold at a profit. He then purchased a church, a parsonage and adjoining building and moved the law school there. He stocked the library with used law books.

He loaded the Board of Trustees and the faculty with conservatives. One of the Trustees was Senator Jesse Helms (dec.) of North Carolina who was later purged by us together with other right-wing conservatives. Some of them were active members of the John Birch Society. By 1972 Charles Vevier (dec.) resigned as President of Adelphi University. In his resignation speech before the Faculty Student Senate he named me as the cause of his resignation. In my view then and now, the University was far better off without him.

At this conservative law school, I felt that it was important to show our diversity. I did not feel that the A.B.A. could look kindly on us if everyone wore jackets and ties. I grew my hair long, had a beard and wore the same jeans every day. I looked like a radical, liberal student from a major undergraduate or graduate school in the 1960's. Students with my appearance were in short supply in the law school.

The students were radicalizing. I ran for the Presidency of the Student Bar Association and won. Avins and some of his faculty would have to be taken out. The school would have to affiliate with a University. The University of Delaware did not want to affiliate with us.

I became friendly with Charles Maddox, the Chairman of Hercules Corporation and our Board of Trustees. Hercules and Du Pont Corporation ran the State. It came down to the summer of 1975, the A.B.A. was considering our Provisional Accreditation. Widener College, just over the border in the State in Pennsylvania had approved our affiliation with them. Now it was up to the A.B.A. The class of 1975 had just graduated and they were hoping for approval so they could take bar examinations. Finally, the call came into the Dean's Office from Charles Maddox. He was calling from the A.B.A. meeting in Hawaii. I was there and he asked to speak with me first. The Class of 75 was outside waiting for a word. Maddox informed me that the A.B.A. had just granted us provisional approval. I handed the phone to the Dean and went outside to inform the students. There was a huge uproar of cheers and applause.

We had phased out Avins relegating him solely to professor status. And had a new Dean, Arthur Weeks (dec.), a southerner with a great track record in dealing with the A.B.A. He had brought Cumberland Law School to accreditation, but the students were really running our school. We published a newspaper which reported cases from the local courts, which then endeared us to the State's lawyers. That was an Avin's idea and our humble student paper became a reporter for decisions from all of the State's courts but especially the Chancery Court, much like the New York Law Journal is to New York lawyers. The Chancery Court in Delaware is a hot bed for corporate litigation nationwide.

We also established a law review, the Delaware Journal of Corporate Law. Since Delaware was considered the "Corporate State", and its Court of Chancery was a mecca of Corporate Law, this too was a great idea by Avins. I and my roommate, Richard Handler became members of the Law Review and published what is called a Student Note in it. The title of the Student Note was: *"A Historical Survey of Federal Incorporation."* It was reprinted in the Congressional Record of the United States as the definitive work on federal incorporation.

I was one of three students honored at the graduation. I should have spoken, but I did not push that envelope. I was out. My parents and Debora Pitman attended. After all was said and done, I became the only student sued by Avins for allegedly colluding with the A.B.A. to remove him as a Dean. He wanted damages. He lost and eventually left the school to start another in Washington, D.C. which did not pan out for him. He died in the early 2000's. After he passed away, I wrote an article about him which was published in the law school's student paper: *"The Smartest and Dumbest Person That I Ever Met."* Avins probably would have been nominated by Ronald Reagan for the Supreme Court of the United States if he had played his cards right.

I thought about staying in Delaware but longed to succeed in the big pond of New York. I have a few innate gifts. All of us have them. The trick is recognizing that we have them; to utilize them for the benefit of ourselves, our family and society at large. It takes some building of confidence and self-esteem. You need to test alternative ways of being, of acting in our daily lives. I do not believe that I was very talented as an athlete, particularly since I had atrial fibrillation, which probably meant that I should have concentrated on my studies in the first place. I may have had an undiagnosed attention deficit disorder (ADHD) because I always made short shrift of school work, until I got to Adelphi, where I developed a love of learning. That is the most important aspect of a university education, developing a love of learning and the ability to think critically.

For some inexplicable reason I have always had a love of writing. To me, the honest expression of the inner self, the realization of ideas that per chance no one else has conceived and the recognition that comes from that is my greatest gift. You might say that I have always been blessed with self-discipline. It is something that I learned in sports. While not talented, I worked harder than anyone else. Work equals rewards, at least some of the time. But when we fail to achieve, when we miss our goals, it should never be for want of trying. When we fail, it is time to get going. As one of the swimming coaches from the University of Michigan once said: "when the going gets tough, the tough get going."

Having faith in myself, having an independent thought process and actions; and above all else, having the will to come back from adversity, to build or re-build is my greatest gift. It is the main ingredient in my life. Self-discipline is the root of all else. It has helped to carry me to overcome the many stressors in my life such as financial issues and criticism by others. My courage in resilience comes from never giving up. I have faith in the worth of all people[1]. Life can be so humbling at times but for me it's all about coming back, negative splitting, making the second part of your life more meaningful than the first part. Setting an example for others to follow is a major part of what I have tried to do in this life. I continue to ask those essential questions of myself, being introspective and of course never getting the answers to the unanswerable questions that I pose to myself. But then I keep going, working harder than anyone else. I believe that there is no one who can or will outwork me. When I compete, my work ethic convinces me that I deserve to win. It gives me stamina and the guts that you need to win.

---

[1] One of my life long friends is Arthur Dobrin, the former Leader of the Ethical Humanist Society of Long Island who married me and Wendy together with a Catholic priest.

Vince Lombardi once said: "Winning is the only thing." I disagree, it is the realization of all things that go with winning or losing that counts.

What you learn in sports about sizing up the opposition and hard work leading to success has transferred to law. Many of my opponents have gone through their lives leading lackluster, mediocre existences. They may be gifted or naturally smart. Many are a lot smarter than I am. But I believe that I am the best at what I do because I came up the hard way, never being given anything on a silver platter. No one can work harder than I do, 24/7. I have taught myself to be a student of human behavior. When I cross examine, it is not just looking for a weak spot in a Q and A, it is looking for weak spots in a witness' demeanor and everything about them. I have heard adversaries describing what I do as "special, as an art form and a gift." I once got a hung jury in a serial rape case because the People's DNA expert had written a Master's Thesis on "opening a lab on a shoestring." I have cross examined a single witness for sixteen days. I have an antenna, that tells me where you are weak, when you cannot look me in the eye, when your voice cracks.

In a medical malpractice case, my experts ran so I had to call the defendant doctor as my first witness, a renowned plastic surgeon from Manhattan. She had an office on Fifth Avenue, across from the Plaza Hotel. My experts sold out to protect one of their own. If I did not call the defendant doctor as my first witness, all would be lost, and I would get sued for malpractice. My client could lose her case. A jury had already been picked. I started by asking this prominent plastic surgeon, how big her office was; the number of employees that she had; the number of patients she had last year; how many surgical procedures she performed and what she charged. When I got done, we were able to show that she was making over five million dollars a year. In front of the jury, she broke down: "Please Judge, tell him to stop, it's not fair." The jury was led out, the case was settled.

In a matrimonial case, the defendant's husband claimed that his business, a prominent beauty salon, was not making any money. I sent my investigator into "shop the place", meaning to check out his price list. We learned that he used three towels per customer and subpoenaed the company that provided him with towels each day. Our forensic accountant then determined his income and profit turned out to be several million dollars. The case settled during the trial.

At the 20th mile of the Boston Marathon, the usual twenty-six-mile race, there is a Heartbreak Hill. It is also referred to as the Wall, which great runners are able to break through. The Wall is a metaphor in all sports and in life itself. In my sport life I was not able to break through the Wall. The Wall is a point where you see the white light of death. Your brain tells you to stop or face certain death. The great athletes say no to death. They go through The Wall. They fight off the pain. Their hearts may be pounding; they can barely lift their arms and legs, but they go on. In life with adversity, it is staring in our faces; when all appears to be lost, it is time to test yourself. Will you break through The Wall? It is a physical, emotional and intellectual test. Each day I ask this of myself. I want to leave a meaningful legacy from which my heirs and others will benefit. Each day through my work and actions I try to set the stage for social change.

In some ways I have found it easier to break through The Wall in life. But one must be given the opportunity or create your own chance. Some of my clients tell me: "Mr. Liotti, you got the game." "Game" means that you're willing to step up to the plate; you're willing to gamble, take a chance and represent clients who are poor and left out. As the musical group The Coasters said: "Some cats got it and other cats ain't."

Oprah Winfrey is a woman with game. Throughout her life she has shown an ability to take on institutions for their elitist, exclusionary policies. Her moving speech at the 2018 Golden Globes further explained her life's story, once as an outsider and now a consummate entrepreneur who has knocked down doors for herself but opened many others for countless women and minorities. She speaks of the culture of change that has brought us from slavery to a pluralistic society, that denounces a return to bigotry. She is now the mountain top.

Chapter XI

Making a Life on My Own

MY FATHER LOUIS was a Democrat whereas my mother Eileen was a Republican. Louis went to church every day. He was member of the Knights of Columbus, the Holy Name Society and an usher for Sunday Masses. My mother was an Episcopalian or Presbyterian, I forget which, no doubt stemming from her deep love of her father Francis Lambe. Francis was born in Glasgow, Scotland. I cannot remember which faith because we never went to a church for either faith. My middle name is Francis, named after him. My first name Thomas is named after my father's father. That is the Italian tradition, to name the first-born son after the paternal grandfather. My mother rarely went to church. As a youth my father would drag me to confessions every Friday night. We also ate only fish on Fridays and fasted for communion on Sundays. Friday's were a treat because we would usually have Pizza from Frank's Pizzeria: "You've tried the Rest, Now Try the Best." The Pizza was half cheese and sauce and the other half was just sauce and anchovies or acciughe. This was my father's preference. The real Italian way to eat Pizza.

There was emphasis on pride in my Italian heritage, less so on the Scottish – Irish side although I still remember attending Irish wakes in the 1950's in Brooklyn where they used to have bars inside the funeral parlors. Today the Irish tailgate their drinking just outside the parlors. My father would say: "Always remember, you're a LIOTTI." Except for him I did not see anything that was terribly prideful about the Liottis'. There was some mention that my paternal grandmother's sister Beatrice Costania had been an opera singer in Italy and that her husband had been an Ambassador. They lived in New Jersey. My paternal grandmother also had two sisters in Italy who I was told were both nuns. My maternal grandfather passed away at the age of seventy-five in 1955, a victim of Parkinson's disease. My paternal grandfather passed away in 1959 at age 69 from a heart disease.

By 1970 I had an interest in politics. What politics would I identify with but Democratic politics and the more liberal side of it. As a union organizer my father clearly had an independent streak in him partly born out of the discrimination that he and other Italians endured. The County of Nassau was controlled for nearly a century by a Republican machine, and by the Party boss Joseph Margiotta (dec.), who would later be indicted, convicted and sent to jail.

My first campaign was for a Democratic State Senate Candidate, Ken Rubenstein. He lost. That was 1970. I became a Democratic Committeeman and eventually a Zone Leader in East Westbury. I was also a member of the New Democratic Coalition (N.D.C.), the liberal wing of the Democratic Party founded by Congressman Allard Lowenstein. From 1970-1972 the goal of the NDC was to chase out of the Democratic Party Committeemen and women who were regular Democrats or what we referred to as Humphreycrats. They were leftover moderate and conservative Democrats who had supported Hubert Humphrey in his 1968 failed campaign for the Presidency against Richard Nixon. We succeeded in ousting the Humphreycrats. The N.D.C. had supported Senator Eugene Mc Carthy and later Bobby Kennedy in 1968 but after 1970 they moved on to support Senator George McGovern for the Presidency. By Fall of 1972 I had moved to Delaware where I worked in Joe Biden's first successful campaign for the United States Senate. I played no other role in Party politics during law school.

During law school I volunteered to work as a Clerk in the Wilmington Legal Aid Society Offices. I was assigned a Landlord / Tenant case. My first assignment took me to an old tenement building in downtown Wilmington. As I opened the front door and stepped into the vestibule, there were rats at my feet. I had never before seen rats. They did not disburse. It was a walk-up apartment and my client screamed at the rats from upstairs. They disbursed, apparently fearful of her murderous intent but otherwise ready to feast upon me. I was fresh or new meat as it were.

It was a walk up building. As I ascended the stairs I noticed the doors to each apartment were cut off at the bottom by three to four inches, no doubt making it easier for the creatures from the vestibule, to make themselves at home inside the apartments. It was winter time and the building had no heat. In visiting my clients, a man and a woman, they were unmarried but living together for convenience. They did not have a refrigerator, so their perishable food was sitting by the window sills between the screens and the windows to stay cold. The woman introduced herself. She had few teeth. On a table nearby, I saw baked beans on soggy white bread. Her male friend was huddled under blankets and clothes on a floor mattress. I gave my report to the Legal Aid Society lawyers whose work I admired but the battles they waged, client by client, apartment by apartment, seemed so hopeless without a change in the mores of society that allowed for such deplorable conditions in the first place. Delaware, the so – called First State, is at the Mason – Dixon Line and was a slave state during the Civil War.

I thought of Bobby Kennedy and his struggle to reach the masses, to change the norms of society. It seemed to me at the time that being a leader who could make fundamental changes in the culture would benefit more people. The work of Legal Aid Lawyers, day to day, had to continue during the transition from bad to a better life for all.

In the late sixties my parents and I had served on the Martin Luther King Jr. Youth Center Board of Directors. Howard Davis's father had recruited us to serve. We were the only Caucasians to serve on the Board and the only people to attend its meetings. Howard Davis won an Olympic Gold Medal in boxing. His father was trying to develop boxing and other programs for the minority community in the poor neighborhood known as New Cassel, next door to the Village of Westbury, where we lived. The Center had few facilities and like other programs in poor neighborhoods was under funded and eventually perished. In its last days it was known as the Kasuri Youth Center.

In my last year of law school, I took a course on legislation and worked in the State Legislature in Dover, Delaware over an hour's drive from Wilmington. I worked one day a week for State Senator Steele (dec.), a legend in the State and a member of the law school's Board of Trustees. He was another hardcore conservative but like many elderly people looking for a stairway to heaven, he had a heart masked by the racist environment in which he grew up. He too eventually favored affiliation with Widener, but it took years of working with him before we could bring him around.

During law school my summers allowed me to return to New York. Irwin always seemed to find work for me somewhere. For two years I was the Pool and Beach Director of the Creek Club where I taught swimming lessons to the children of the very rich and famous. At night I traveled to the estates of the North Shore and taught private swimming lessons in those pools. I saw a contrast between the poor and the wealthy but I was in the middle class. Would I gravitate toward the wealthy or the poor or simply remain locked in with a middle-class existence?

A memorable act of rebellion against the upper class occurred while at the Creek Club. It and the Piping Rock Club, its neighbor, are among the most elite Clubs in the nation, keeping out all minorities from their memberships. One summer while at the Creek an elderly member kept saying that no one had swam across the Sound since his son did so in 1936. So, in August of 1974, my friend Terry Laughlin (dec.) and I decided to swim across Long Island Sound from Greenwich, Connecticut to Oyster Bay. We borrowed a pilot boat from a member which broke down in Connecticut. We made the swim, a distance of about nine miles without a pilot boat. It took us three hours and forty-five minutes. We made our way through the schools of blue fish, brown sharks, power and other boats that nearly ran us down.

In the summer of 1975, I had four jobs. I was helping to coach Irwin's swimmers at the Garden City Pool from 6 a.m. to 8 a.m. after that I drafted legal papers for a law firm in Garden City, it was my first legal job. In the evening I would return to the Garden City Pool for an adult swim class. I taught adults how to swim except for one gentleman, 87. I taught him how to float.

On the one day that I had off each week I worked as a volunteer in the local jail. I thought that I might be a criminal defense attorney, like Perry Mason. But I had never been around alleged criminals before and I thought that I might be afraid of them. I was assigned to the library and recreation programs. The legal books in the library were all outdated. The teacher assigned to the jail from the nearby School District never showed. The inmates were eager to learn how to read but there was no one to teach them, I did the best I could, with no facilities or teaching aids.

I ate with the guards. One day I was in the Recreation Yard. It was all asphalt with four high prison walls around us. An inmate had a seizure. The guard on duty did nothing while I helped the inmate out of it. He was never given any meds or sent to the infirmary. He was just sent back up to his tier. I wrote a report about my experiences and gave it over to the District Attorney. The next year nineteen guards were indicted for abuses and corruption at the jail.

Once out of law school I had to take the Bar Exam. I had been my law school's representative for the Practicing Law Institute. So, I qualified for a free bar review course. Each morning during the summer of 1976 I took my bar review course at Hofstra University School of Law; studied at home and in the evening at C.W. Post, Long Island University in Brookville. I had also been teaching Economics at Delaware Technical and Community College. This was the same school in which Jill Biden, the former Vice President's wife taught and administered. Back in New York I was isolated. Just studying with nothing to show for it is grinding. The world around you is filled with people who have purpose whereas your only purpose is to pass the Bar Exam so that you may one day have a purpose. You must read and study for hours each day, every day. It is repetitive and boring. Every Sunday I took a legal writing class in New York City.

At the time before multi – state bar exams came into existence; I had attended what was referred to as a national law school whereas New York law schools such as St. John's emphasized New York Law throughout their curriculum. National schools focused on federal law giving the local schools an advantage in taking the New York Bar Exam. Since the Bar Exam was given in July, I had to learn New York Law in six weeks. At the time, the New York Bar Exam tested in forty subject areas with emphasis on New York Civil practice and evidence.

But no one told me that, so I studied all forty areas even though subjects like labor law were hardly tested if at all.

On Sunday mornings I took a writing class in Manhattan in preparation for the Bar Exam's twelve essays. In the midst of my preparation, I was offered a position with the New York City Legal Aid Society in their Criminal Law Division and the Legal Services Corporation in Washington, D.C. practicing civil law. Both jobs involved representing the poor which was an area of interest to me.

While I was interviewed and waiting for Bar Exam results, I took a job at a downtown New York City law firm as a Law librarian and Junior Associate. A partner in that firm lived on Park Avenue for six months out of the year and in Paris for the other six months. He was chauffeured downtown to the office each day. There was a chef in the firm whose sole job was to cook breakfast for him, served with copies of the Wall Street Journal. This partner had rules. One rule was you could not have your jacket off in the common areas of the firm and if you did so, you did it in your office and your door had to be closed. An addition to that rule was you must never have your jacket off in the presence of a client. Another rule was that you had to reshelve your books. We had been working on a project for the Nigerian Government. In the days of book research as opposed to computerized research we had books open and marked for cases. They were stacked about three feet high on two conference tables. I had been staying at the Downtown New York Athletic Club while working on the project until 11 p.m. and returning at 7 a.m.

Near the project's end we went out for lunch to celebrate, leaving our books out awaiting our return for the writing part of the project. While we were out the partner who ordinarily took his lunch at the Wall Street Club reshelved our books, killing a month of research time. Upon returning I hand wrote a letter of resignation, placed it on another partner's desk and walked out. I did not have a job but I had hope while waiting for the Bar results.

The Bar results came out in December. They were published in the New York Times. You had to go to Times Square to get the early edition, hot off the press. I went with my mother and did not pass. All of that work seemed like a terrible waste. I still did not have a job and did not feel that I should take the job offered to me by Legal Aid or the Legal Services Corporation although I could have because new hires were allowed to take the Bar Exam more than once without being terminated.

A Law Professor friend, was taking a Master in Law Degree Program at New York University. She encouraged me to move into the City. I enrolled in the N.Y.U. Master of Tax Law program, so I could study for the Bar there and live in the N.Y.U. Law School Dormitory, right off of Washington Square Park, in the heart of Greenwich Village. I took the subway each day up to mid-town for a Bar Review course with Joe Marino. I went to Joe's office in Garden City after failing the Bar. I said to him: "Will I ever pass?" he told me that I would; that I had over studied, ignoring what was most important: "You see that guy over there? He failed the Bar 57 times. He works for me." At that time if you failed the Bar, you could go to Albany and copy down the questions and correct answers to the Bar Exam, I had done that. The questions and answers were repeated so Marino had the book on all the questions and answers. "Just take notes on everything I say and keep reading them." At the end of six weeks at 3-4 hours per day I had 4000 pages of notes which I read over three times. Sure enough when I took the Bar the second time out of the twelve essays, Marino hit on eight of them. I regurgitated what he said. By March I had taken the exam and returned to Long Island.

Chapter XII

Meeting Wendy and Start of my Legal Career

WHILE I WAS studying at N.Y.U. I met Wendy, my future wife. Some years earlier I had seen her and had been her and her brother Eddy's swim coach. She had graduated from Carle Place High School in 1972. She was number two in her class with a 99 average. She was Salutatorian. She could have attended any school in the country but decided to attend Duke University, at first as a pre-med student, then into the School of Nursing because she could not stand the sight of blood. Later she became Fine Arts major, graduating with honors in 1976.

She was taking a course on retail marketing at N.Y.U. when I ran into her in the neighborhood one day. Her car battery had broken down. We finally got to a firehouse in the Village and got her battery jumped. After that she became my life line to the civilized world outside of schools and academia. She would somehow find me every week in the catacombs of the subterranean stacks in the basements of the law school or in the massive stacks of the undergraduate library. I don't know how she did it. We would have coffee together at Le Figaro Café, an old beatnik hangout from the 50's and 60's, at the corner of Bleecker and MacDougal Streets, where Bob-Dylan, Peter, Paul and Mary and others got their start near and at the Bitter End Café; Cafe Wha? and the Village Gate.

The N.Y.U. Law School was among the top five in the United Sates. It's Master's in Tax Law program was number one. Students from all over the world came there to study. The Tax law professor from my law school was there to earn a second Master's in Tax Law degree.

In any event that's not why I was there. I was there to study for the Bar exam and that is all I did, day and night. I did attend some of the tax classes but had no time to read the enormous tax code and accompanying regulations. I left N.Y.U. without completing the program.

The Bar Exam was in February. Each day my routine would consist of jogging around Washington Square Park and swimming in the law school's dormitory pool which was just off the Park. There was a steam bath there which would also allow me to be idle for a few minutes. Once the Bar Exam was over, I abandoned the Tax program and my dorm room, returning to my parent's home, still unemployed and closing in on my thirtieth birthday.

I decided that I wanted to run for office returning to my Democratic roots. I was convinced that I would practice in Long Island but needed name recognition in order to attract clients. I was hoping to pass the Bar, but I was not viewing myself as a practicing lawyer. I wanted to be an elected official, a leader who would promote social change in the fabric of our society, just like the Kennedys, Martin Luther King Jr., Ralph Nader, and Allard Lowenstein had. They were reformers. I wanted to do what they had done.

I wanted to run for Supervisor in the Town of North Hempstead. It had a population of about 240,000. I would run against Mike Tully (dec.), the Republican / Conservative standard bearer as a Democratic / Independent candidate. The Republicans had been in power for almost a hundred years. The "Republican Machine" was the best one in the nation. It was headed by Joseph Margiotta (dec.), a notorious figure who later went to jail for receiving a portion of the municipal insurance premiums which he controlled. His Tammany Hall type system also required municipal employees to kick back to the GOP one percent of their annual salary. That oiled the machine until it was revealed in the early 1980's and the Party had to pay back more than one million dollars to the workers.

I did not have a job, so all I did was campaign, all day every day. My father had given $15,000.00 to the campaign. We had saved a little money beyond that for some literature. Aside from a few Democrats in the County Committee, I really had a skeleton staff.

My father Louis did everything he could. My future wife Wendy was also there every step of the way. My friend Neal Belmuth was a brilliant, high tech guy from Great Neck. He designed an attaché case that played John Philip Sousa music which we used at railroad stations. We had a limited budget with only 10,000 pieces of literature. At railroad stations commuters would come by, we would hand out the literature and just as quickly as we gave them the brochures they would say: "Democrat!" and proceed to throw it into the trash. In between trains we would retrieve the brochures from the trash and give it out to the next wave of commuters. It was our own recycling program.

I was asked to give the main address at the annual dinner of the County Committee. I introduced my running mate, the County Executive candidate, to rousing applause. Irwin Landes (dec.) was a graduate of Harvard College and its Law School. He had been an Assemblyman for seven years. He was from North Hempstead and very popular among Democrats especially those in the Jewish communities. While ordinarily I would not have a prayer of winning against "The Machine", Irwin's coat tails in North Hempstead were a big deal. On the campaign trail people would come up to me and give me checks for Irwin. I felt that we were closing. Five weeks before Election Day Irwin was trailing his Republican opponent by just three percentage points. Since his main strength would come from North Hempstead, I had an outside chance of victory.

But then the shoe fell. The media as a result of leaks provided to them by "The Machine," found that while Irwin had graduated from Harvard Law School, he had practiced law for twenty-four years without a license. He had passed the Bar Exam but never went through an interview with the Character and Fitness Committee, the last step in the approval process before admission to the Bar.

While this revelation was daunting enough the Republicans then found out that he had not filed tax returns for a number of years. This too was reported in the media. After that we could not get Irwin out of bed. He was later prosecuted and convicted.

I continued to campaign, but lost, not badly though. I interviewed with the Nassau District Attorney but did not get the job most likely because the District Attorney perceived me as a potential threat since his office policy was that assistants could not be involved in politics. I had been involved in politics in a big way and thus he viewed me as a potential challenger to his position.

Angelo Orazio was my local Assemblyman. He was a Democrat. I put out my feelers to him for a position in the Albany State Legislature. I still did not have a job, but right after Election Day, Wendy and I decided to get married.

On December 17, 1977, we were married at the United States Merchant Marine Academy Chapel, on a beautiful day overlooking Long Island Sound. Performing the ceremony was Arthur Dobrin, Ph.D., the leader of the Ethical Humanist Society of Long Island and a Catholic priest whose name I do not recall. My father said he would not attend the ceremony unless there was a priest so we had one from the Academy. Edgar Kendricks (dec.) from the Sesame Street Television show and known as the Mayor of Harlem sang beautifully and the Manhasset String Ensemble, fifty wonderful children all dressed in white turtle necks and red vests, played magnificently on their violins. My best Man was Bill Irwin, my former coach and best friend. Our reception for two hundred plus people, was held at Plandome Country Club. Our wedding song was theme from the movie The Godfather.

Wendy and I went on our honeymoon to Eleuthera in the Bahamas. It was terrible, the weather was not good and the place at which we stayed was called the Current Club. We renamed it the Past Club. Its features included a ping pong table with three legs and one paddle and a boat for scuba diving which never left the dock but billowed smoke each morning as its Captain unsuccessfully attempted to engineer its launching. The cuisine was also special - conch served for breakfast, lunch and dinner each day.

We came back to New York with only a few dollars left over from the wedding money. We had no furniture or a place to stay. My mother-in-law owned a building with her sister on a main street in the center of the town. The tenants were moving out of the first floor, so we moved in and it had five rooms. It was an old building built in 1920. We lived in it for about a year and a half. I was putting a sign outside for my law office, and started taking cases from the community. My mother-in-law had a real estate office next door and all the Italians knew her. She was like Mafia Don. None of them would make a move without talking to "Mrs. Carole". She is from the Bronx, one hundred percent Italian.

We both worked for the community as volunteers. Wendy is seven and half years younger than me. She was in the League of Women voters and writing a weekly column for the local paper. She was also getting her Master's Degree in Fine Arts at Pratt Institute in Brooklyn. She taught Calculus in the local high school and got a job in a private all-girls school in Garden City, which has since closed. She also Founded the Cathedral School Art Academy, an after-school program where she taught art to children in the community. We did fundraisers for the March of Dimes and the American Cancer Society. I joined Kiwanis and eventually became its President. In addition to practicing law, I was also teaching Business Law at New York Institute of Technology. Together we ran as Co-Directors, the Frog Hollow Frolics for three years. It was a series of vaudeville acts by people in the community to raise money for scholarships for deserving youngsters.

My first client was New Again Construction Company which I unofficially renamed, Sued Again Construction Company. They gave us a rental apartment above their office – a four room apartment in a house which they were using illegally for their office. We bought a bed and Wendy felt it was essential that we have a stereo. That essentially exhausted the wedding money. We really had no other furniture. If we had friends or family over, we would put a table cloth down on the floor. We had a mouse problem which Wendy kept at bay. We nicknamed her "The Hunter."

I borrowed a desk and chair from New Again. I set up a make shift office in the house in which I could never have any clients visit. I had an orange extension cord which went across a bare wood floor. It was connected to the used I.B.M. Selectric Typewriter which I bought for fifty dollars. My chair did not have a bottom in it. I did not know how to type, so after playing with that for a while I found a typist who I took work to each day, picking it up in the afternoons and paying her cash. My one room office contained an unusable bathroom in one of the four rooms of our apartment. The rent was $350.00 per month.

I had been elected to be our County delegate to the mid-term Democratic National Convention in 1978 but the Democrats were otherwise not taking care of me. I was struggling in my practice. My mother in law was in the real estate business and started to send me business. I was still doing mostly small transactional work. A local electrician started giving me some work but I still had an interest in politics. Since we only had one car, clients drove me to the court which involved mostly Small Claims cases. I was waiting for the Democrats to do something but nothing was happening. I was thirty-one and anxious to make a move.

As I look back on my life, I have some regrets, as many of us do, about my personal development. While my adoptive parents were spectacular people, I wish they had been more of an inspiration to me academically. Aside from sports I really never had any hobbies. My father did not read books. My mother did but usually biographies. I was never taken to museums or Broadway shows. I never traveled much in the United States and never outside of it until I went to a Mexican border town after the 1968 Olympic Team Trials. I was not raised with a world view, a weltanschauung or even a metropolitan view. I was raised in a provincial, suburban setting. When my father bought the Sunday paper which he would always give me to read and I did, it was usually Newsday, the Daily News and the New York Post. It was not the New York Times, which I now read every day.

I was never read to or asked to write anything. We never had discussions about music or art. I never played an instrument. I was never taken to the woods to appreciate the birds and wild life there. I never appeared in a play. It was not that my parents intentionally deprived me of these cultural accoutrements. They were brought up during the Great Depression, so they never had these experiences. They could not impart them to me because they did not know of them. I am hopeful that my children who were given a broader experience when they were growing up will impart a broader academic and cultural experience to their children. My children, thanks mostly to my wife, have had some of the elements of a more diversified life experience. While it was a financial struggle for us, all three of my children attended a private school before going to college.

Our first children, twins were born on May 25, 1985, at Columbian Presbyterian Hospital in Manhattan, Louis Joseph, named after my father and Carole Lynne was named after my mother-in-law and taking Wendy's middle name as her own. Francesca Eileen was born four years later on April 30, 1989. She is named after Wendy's grandmother and my mother.

Like every generation, we were trying to do better by our children so they all started in an elite pre-school program. We did everything with them. We joined an exclusive South Shore Beach Club and were house members of a prestigious North Shore Country Club.

All three graduated from college without student loans. My son Louis attended the Green Vale School, pre-K through eighth grade. He then attended Portledge Prep School and thereafter Northeastern University on an 85 percent scholarship for hockey. My daughter Francesca attended the same school pre – K through ninth grade and then attended and graduated from the Pomfret Preparatory School in Connecticut. Thereafter, she graduated from the University of Denver. My daughter Carole, Louis' twin, attended Green Vale pre – K through 4th grade and then switched to the Carle Place Public Schools. She graduated from Adelphi University.

All of our children were involved in sports programs. Louis was a superb hockey player; Carole was an outstanding figure skater who spent six summers at the Olympic Training Center in Lake Placid and Francesca was an equestrian with her own horse, Elvis, who definitely had a mind of his own.

Our home which we have lived in for 40 years in Westbury has been expanded and built up from its original four rooms. We had live-in housekeepers for 12 years and our children took every lesson you can think of: tennis, violin, surfing, chess with a master teacher, Little League, swimming and soccer.

An old friend of mine, and fabulous attorney Michael Kennedy, Esq. (dec.), once advised: "Live right, think left!" This probably sums up my life. My adoptive parents were hardworking, honest people. To a certain extent they let me evolve on my own but I am sure that some of their wonderful character traits rubbed off on me. I owe them a good outcome where I benefit others as they benefited me. If not for them I would have been a ward of the state; a homeless person or in jail. I recognize that some of us are luckier than others. I was very lucky.

Chapter XIII

Discoveries and Reunions
By: Mary Sirchia (cousin)

2017 SAW MOMENTOUS changes to my family tree. Thanks to science and technology, two lost babies have been reunited with their respective families. Two children, now adults, from different sides of my family have found their way into our hearts.

In September 2017, I noted a new entry on my Ancestry relatives list. Thomas Liotti. A surname I was not familiar with, yet he was listed as a second cousin. I did not respond right away. I was curious but wary. Who was Thomas Liotti?? I needed to know my mysterious second cousin. The mystery thickened when I asked him to share his family tree and he responded by suggesting I read his book, "The Secret Adoption".

The first thought that ran through my head was the adoption story I had heard just a few years before. A story of a cousin giving birth to a baby and giving it away. It was a family secret that was kept from me and my siblings as probably too scandalous for our tender ears. The baby was born on May 29, 1947. I bought the book and hungrily read every word as though I was discovering a hidden treasure. There it was, the proof that my cousin Ann, did indeed give birth to a son and six days later gave him away. In his book, Tom revealed that he didn't find out that he was adopted until he was 60 years old. I can imagine the shock this must have been for him. His entire life turned upside down. He was not who he thought he was. He was, but he wasn't.

After reading the details of his search for his identity, and the findings of his private investigator, I saw that some of the details were correct, but some were glaringly wrong. The investigator had erred and gone down the wrong path due to their being several potential leads with the same name. I was beside myself with joy and realization that I was reading about our "lost baby". Who to call with the news first?? I couldn't contain myself.

Here is a copy of the message I forwarded to my new cousin Tom:

Dear cousin,

As you suggested, I read your book "The Secret Adoption". Without a doubt we are related on my maternal side. I want to say immediately how fortunate you were to be adopted by such a loving couple that cared so much for you. Your biological mother would not or could not have provided for you financially or emotionally.

Your private investigator got some of the information wrong, but mostly right. Your mother, Anne Ferguson married John (Jack) Smith. They had one son named John Richard. The marriage was not a happy one and they separated. I do not know if there was a divorce. Anne Ferguson was known as Anne Smith, that was her legal name. She moved from Brooklyn to Lynbrook, L.I. NY. She was not a nurse. She also never lived in Cleveland, Ohio. She did eventually move to Stroudsburgh, Pennsylvania. where she died.

There is so much more I could tell you but you also have a first cousin living in Lynbrook, L.I. Her name is Eileen King. She would be able to give you more information.

I am so happy that you have contacted a member of your family through Ancestry.com I know this message is brief and very inadequate, but it is a start.

Recently, through Ancestry.com, my children were united with their half-sister. As a result, I now have a step grandson who is someone you probably know. His name is Gregory Grizopoulus. Small world.

This last paragraph is a good lead in to the second child that has been found. But before I begin that story, I have to complete my thoughts on Tom's adoption:

No mother gives her child away lightly. You were carried in your mother's womb for nine months. You were given life. Whatever her thoughts, whatever her anguish, only she knows her reasons. We, her family can only speculate and we would probably be wrong. Anne Ferguson Smith, your mother, had a failed marriage, a troubled son born 9 years earlier and a bleak future for her new baby. Under the circumstances I think Anne Smith did what turned out to be in your very best interest. Unless you have walked in another's shoes you cannot judge…

No matter the circumstances of your adoption, thanks to your loving and nurturing adoptive parents you are a successful attorney, husband, and father. Whether Prince or Pauper, you are family.

Tom, you had an older brother named John Richard Smith. He has passed away, but left you nieces and a nephew. You are an uncle. In the Fall of 2017, we held a family reunion where you and your wife Wendy could meet your new family. We gathered together as many cousins as we could get as well as our new member of the family and her children.

You should know something of the family in which you find yourself. We are mostly middle-class America. Our occupations range from Ph. Ds, a rocket scientist, nurses, firefighter, policeman, librarian, teacher, MBA's, and stockbrokers. We are of Irish stock that have married Germans, Italians, African-Americans, Latino's, and Scandinavians.

Your Grandmother Ellen Erwin and my Grandfather Thomas Erwin were part of a larger Erwin family that originally came from Scotland, but then branched out to Ireland. We are proud of our Irish heritage, but are first and foremost patriotic Americans, mostly conservative Republicans with a sprinkling of Democrats. We march in the St. Patrick's Day parade every year and soccer is our game.

So, welcome to our family. We look forward to many future occasions where we can celebrate our holidays, and special family days.

In the Spring of 2017, my children met and welcomed a half-sister into the family. Her name is Star. Yes, that is her real name. John Sirchia, who was to be my future husband, was her father. This took place before I met or knew him. Later, I was to learn of her existence but there was never any contact.

Star was sixteen years old when she accidentally found out that the man, she called Dad was really a step-father. Her real father's name was John Sirchia, the man that would later become my future husband.

I met my husband John when we were Art students at Pratt Institute in Brooklyn, NY.

Eventually, when we became a serious item, he told me that he knew he had a daughter, but he had no contact with her. Star was raised by her mother who was Greek, and a step father who was Italian.

Fast forward to 2017. Star is now 68 years old and, her mother has passed away. She is beginning to think it may be time to search for her biological father. She is reluctant to begin, but her daughter took on an active role and eventually made contact with her mother's half-brother, my son Tom. The rest is history and by July of that same year a reunion took place on Long Island. Brothers and sisters were happily united. They are delighted with each other. Star has two children, Kara and Gregory. Gregory is John Sirchia's grandson and the spitting image of him, so much so that it brought tears to my eyes. She said she had always wondered what her father looked like, and didn't realize she was looking at him in her son. I am happy that my children have a piece of their father in Star. She is a gift.

It seems that I am the catalyst in both reunions. There is a photo of a family reunion that took place in 1982. On the left side of the picture is my husband, Star's father. Toward the right side of the picture is Tom Liotti's mother, my cousin Ann. Both in the same picture unknown to each other that 35 years later they would be drawn together by an inquiry into Ancestry.com.

As for me, what are my thoughts? I love Star as a daughter. She calls me Mother Mary.

She is a delight to talk to. My boys love their new sister. My daughter speaks daily to her.

Star's son Gregory is an attorney on Long Island and knows Tom Liotti through the courts. Tom discovered he is mostly Irish and British and not Italian. His mother Ann, my cousin, would be surprised that I would be the instrument to bring Tom back to his family. Life is strange and interesting. You never know who is beside you.

Epilogue

MY NEW FAMILY, as I call them is filled with loving people, who have welcomed me. The rejection that I may have felt in first learning of my adoption has now been overcome to a significant extent by their acceptance. They do not blame me for the miscarriages created by my natural mother, father, and older brother. I have no doubt that my life was far better being raised by my adoptive parents than it would have been had I been raised by irresponsible, neglectful and indifferent natural parents. I do not think this is too harsh because natural parents have a responsibility to their offspring once bringing them into the world. Without exemplary guidance and leadership, the young if left on their own to develop, will be forced to fend for themselves in every way meaning ideologically and in their lifestyles. Abraham Lincoln was an exception. He was educated up until the age of 9, when his mother died and his father left Abe and his younger sister alone in a small cabin of rural Illinois while he went to search for a new wife. As a ward of the State, I do not know what I would have become – a laborer, a hardened criminal, homeless, sick, or uneducated with a shortened life expectancy.

What I missed is not the love of natural parents because mine were apparently incapable of that, but the love that my new family is so very capable of giving and have given to me. They did not have to do that. Mary Sirchia did not have to search for or find me. Yet she is such a remarkable person, a figurehead and leader in the family, that others have shown their respect for her incredible efforts. She is a quiet heroine not just to me but to millions of lost or adopted children.

We cannot turn back the clock or make up for lost love. I grew up without much of an extended family and now I have one. They are used to having a large, extended family, all being close. I have to make adjustments to become a better family member. That means learning more about the family history. This is an attempt at that. When I was first found and welcomed into the family, they made me feel like a star but once blended into their lives and theirs into mine, I will no doubt learn more about being a member of my new family. We're still just getting acquainted and introduced after seventy years of not knowing one another. We are evolving and while the passage of time cannot heal all wounds, it can also point to new beginnings. A world of peace and love can begin with what we give and receive in our own families.

The loneliness that I felt as an adopted, only child without an extended family will always be a part of me but while I was lucky to have been adopted, I am lucky a second time being adopted by my new family. It has been an easier transition for me than it may be for them because I did not know my natural parents whereas my loving new family endured the negatives that my natural parents and older brother presented. I have only reconstructed memories of them as told to me by new family members. But they had those actual experiences, some of which are pretty awful. I suggest that it is going to be easier for me to put this limited knowledge behind me than it will be for my new family to do so, since they lived through it. I feel some obligation to make up for the negativity in their lives that may have been caused by my natural parents and older brother. I want to forget them but probably will not be able to erase them from my memory. Their genes are mine. I cannot change that, but my own life, thanks to nurturing by exceptional adoptive parents has followed and will follow a very different path. Thankfully it is a path of love and peace which my new family exemplifies.

I cannot speak for all adopted people, only for myself but I am happy that I did not learn of my adoption until I was sixty years of age and the identity of my natural parents at seventy years of age.

My search for them was based upon wanting to learn more about their health rather than any real curiosity about their lives. I determined early on that they were probably pretty dull, boring and mediocre people whose lives were not distinguished in anyway. Except for what I might learn about them genetically which might help my children, I had no other pragmatic interest in them. I felt no identity with them but for obvious reasons. My adoptive parents were so much better as people. They have a quiet legacy and me because I bear their name. But there is nothing to account for the lives of my natural parents. It is as if they never existed. I confess to having a resentment for people whose lives are just about themselves. Given the goodness that I have seen in my new family, it appears that my natural parents were barely part of it. Their memory will take up a very tiny place in my brain almost like any Post Office photo but probably never rising to the level of a notable obituary.

I live each day to take what experiences I can out of it. I strive to do something for the mind and body each day. I strive to add to my legacy, to my experiences. Clumsily I strive to change the world one case and one person at a time. I have painstakingly learned that the more I give, the more I get back. I want to give more to all because while I am grateful to have found my family, I feel that I have a larger family also. It is my truest family. It is the same one that each of us has. It is the family of this world and everyone in it, living, dead and yet to be born. It is this galaxy and all beyond it. Being reunited with this new family does not mean that I have abandoned my older one or that it is passé. Rather my new family is part of me just as the old one is. So is the extended family, meaning all in this world, before this and after it. I embrace all of you, living, dead and yet to be born, now and forever.

The Mitochondrial DNA test on Thomas F. Liotti and Anne C. Ferguson

THIS TEST WAS based upon information given by Joan Dinneen, from Port Washington, New York. She believed she knew Anne Ferguson (the author's mother) who was mentioned in the Newsday article on January 29, 2012 at page 20 and 21. This DNA test was performed to determine if Anne C. Ferguson and Thomas F. Liotti were of the same maternal lineage. They were not and it was determined this Anne C. Ferguson was not related.

The Ancestry previous and updated DNA results were the catalyst that led Mary Sirchia to find her cousin, Thomas F. Liotti.

Introduction to Photographs

Mary Sirchia was instrumental in providing the photographs beginning with Jack Smith and Anne Ferguson's wedding. In this photographic journey the author introduces members of his family and their relationship to him. It culminates with a joyful celebration reuniting the author and his wife with the family that was kept from him through a secret held in the hearts of his adoptive parents and finally revealed through a birthday gift and the love of a daughter who assisted in a father's quest for the truth.

Mitochondrial DNA Test

GENETICA
DNA Test

Genetica DNA
Laboratories, Inc.

Montgomery Rd

Cincinnati, Ohio

U S A

ORDER IDENTITY

	Alleged Relative #1	Alleged Relative #2
Case No. 97342		
Run # mtDNA_43		
Patient Name	Thomas F. Liotti	Anne C. Ferguson
Date of Birth	May 29, 1947	March 30, 1951
Race	American	Caucasian
Date Collected	June 22, 2012	June 15, 2012
Test Number	97342-41	97342-42
Mitochondrial Region	Differences from rCRS	Differences from rCRS
HV-1	16,193 T	16,172 C
16,024 - 16,365	16,219 G	16,193 T
	16,362 C	16,223 T
		16,278 T
		16,390 A
HV-2	93 G	73 G
73 - 340	204 C	89 C
	239 C	93 G
	263 C	95 C
	309.1 C (insertion)	146 C
	315.1 C (insertion)	150 T
		152 C
		182 T
		195 C
		263 G
		309.1 C (insertion)
		315.1 C (insertion)
		325 T
MATERNAL LINEAGE LIKELIHOOD RATIO	0	

Report Date: July 20, 2012

Interpretation of Results:

Specimens from Thomas F. Liotti and Anne C. Ferguson were submitted for DNA analyses to determine the likelihood that Thomas F. Liotti shares the same maternal lineage as Anne C. Ferguson. The mitochondrial DNA HV-1 and HV-2 regions of Thomas F. Liotti are different from the revised Cambridge Reference Sequence (rCRS) at the following positions: 16,193 T, 16,219 G, 16,362 C, 93 G, 204 C, 239 C, 263 C, 309.1 C insertion, and 315.1 C insertion. The mitochondrial DNA HV-1 and HV-2 regions of Anne C. Ferguson are different from the revised Cambridge Reference Sequence (rCRS) at the following positions: 16,172 C, 16,193 T, 16,223 T, 16,278 T, 16,390 A, 73 G, 89 C, 93 G, 95 C, 146 C, 150 T, 152 C, 182 T, 195 C, 263 G, 309.1 C insertion, 315.1 C insertion and 325 T. Therefore, the data shows that the mitochondrial DNA sequences of Thomas F. Liotti and Anne C. Ferguson DO NOT MATCH and are NOT consistent with individuals who share a common maternal lineage.

Subscribed and sworn before me on July 20, 2012.

Kimberly L. Marto
Notary Public, State of Ohio
My Commission Expires: 4/25/2018

I, Elizabeth Panke, M.D., Ph.D., verify that the interpretation of results is correct as reported and the above testing was conducted in accordance with the recommended guidelines for DNA testing set forth by AABB.

Elizabeth Panke, M.D., Ph.D.
Laboratory Director

You deserve the very best, request...the GENETICA DNA Test™

Previous Estimate

Ireland/Scotland/Wales	54%
Europe West	34%
Scandinavia	4%
Europe South	3%
Great Britain	2%
Caucasus	1%
Iberian Peninsula	<1%
Finland/Northwest Russia	<1%
Europe East	<1%

Updated Estimate

● **Ireland & Scotland** Increased by 14%	**68%**
● **England, Wales & Northwestern Europe** Increased by 30%	**32%**

Additional Communities

- **Connacht, Ireland**
  - North Connacht
  - North Mayo
  - North East Mayo & North West Sligo
- **Leinster, Ireland**
  - Wicklow, Carlow & Wexford

Jack Smith and Anne Ferguson's Wedding
(author's biological parents).

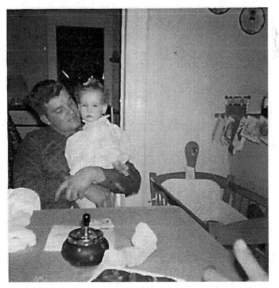

John Smith and Father John "Jack" Smith

John Smith with daughter Christine, December, 1962.

Anne Ferguson Smith and granddaughter Christine.

September, 1963, Anne Ferguson with granddaughter Christine.

Thomas F. Liotti's mother Anne Ferguson
with granddaughter Christine

Thomas F. Liotti's mother Anne Ferguson with Eileen
King's Daughters, Kelly Ann and Erin Eileen.

This photo was taken in 1982, shows my mother Anne Ferguson, seated in the second-row center; her sister Eileen is one over, second form the right side of the photo in the second row. John Sirchia is in the second row on the end of the left side of the photo. Mary Sirchia is just behind John in the back row.

First arrival at the reunion party and seeing photos
of mother and father for the first time.

Thomas F. Liotti with his 2nd cousin Mary
Sirchia, who found him on Ancestry.com

(Left to Right) Star; Robert; Kim Redmond, married
to Patrick; Wendy, author's wife; Mary, Author,
Eileen King; Patrick Redmond and Lynne
Ranaghan (Mary's daughter).

(Left to Right) Mary; Author; Patrick Redmond,
Mary's brother's son and Eileen King.

(Left to Right) Lynne Ranaghan, Mary's daughter;
Eileen King, 1st cousin; author and Mary.

(Left to Right) Robert Sirchia, Mary's son; Lynne
Marie Sirchia, Robert's daughter; Mary;
Elizabeth Sirchia, Robert's wife and author.

Kara, Mary and Author.

Thomas F. Liotti with his 1st cousin Eileen King on the left,
on the right is his niece Christine and grand niece Ashley

John Sirchia (Mary Sirchia's husband)

Star and Robert.

(Left to Right) Author; Gregory Grizopoulos;
Mary and Star Rochenbucher.

Thomas F. Liotti and Gregory Grizopoulos, grandson of John Sirchia.

Cousins gathered to welcome Tom and Wendy
into the family, November, 2017.

September 1, 2018, Louis and Megan's wedding day in Jersey
City, New Jersey with the Manhattan skyline in the background.
(Left to Right) Carole L. Liotti, Francesca E. Liotti, Megan Greth
Liotti, Louis J. Liotti, Wendy L. Liotti and Thomas F. Liotti

The author in October, 2018 at Babe Ruth's gravesite at the Gate
To Heaven Cemetery in Hawthorne, New York. Babe Ruth was
an orphan. As an adoptee the author identifies with and is inspired
by #3 as a New York Yankee. He was the "Great Bambino" and
the "King of Swat" (1895-1948) not just because of his 60 home
runs or 714 life time, but because he was a "larger than life" figure
who cared deeply about people and children in particular.

QUEST
TO FIND HIS
ROOTS

LI man sought birth parents after learning at 60 that he was adopted

BY ANN GIVENS
ann.givens@newsday.com

Frail, sick and angry that his son was moving him to an assisted-living facility, Louis Liotti said something at the end of his life five years ago that he could never take back.

"You are not my son," Liotti told the man, then 60, that he and his wife had raised since infancy.

Something in the way the ailing 91-year-old said it made Thomas Liotti, a Garden City lawyer and Westbury Village justice, know that it was true. The news sent Liotti on a mission to find himself and to learn about the birthparents he had never known.

"I had to reconceive who I really am," Liotti said in a recent interview. "Everything I thought I was was suddenly pulled out from under me."

This month, Liotti published a book about his search called "The Secret Adoption." The book, which he self-published through iUniverse, is available through Amazon.com and BarnesandNoble.com.

By Liotti's own account, the December 2007 revelation that he had been adopted sent him into a tailspin. After all, he had been president of the Columbian Lawyers' Association of Nassau County, a professional group for lawyers of

Thomas Liotti and parents on book cover.

Italian heritage. Now it appeared he may not have been Italian at all, but Irish and maybe English.

"When you find out you're adopted, there's a longing and search for identity," said John Pessala, a 30-year friend of Liotti's and a retired Nassau Family Court judge who often speaks publicly about his own adoption. "You are searching for your identity: religious, national, psychological and, of course, medical. Simply stated, it's who you are."

The obvious people for Liotti to ask about his past — his adoptive mother and father were little help. His adoptive mother, Eileen, 88, was already suffering from advanced Alzheimer's disease in 2007 and could neither fill in the blanks about his past nor explain her own motives or feelings about it.

Louis Liotti, the son of Italian immigrants and a World War II veteran, said little about the reason he and his wife had adopted, Thomas Liotti said. Louis Liotti said his wife suffered as many as seven miscarriages.

"I think it was really shattering for both of them," Thomas Liotti said.

At last, the elder Liotti told his son that they were approached by the superintendent of their Brooklyn apartment building, who said he knew a young woman who was pregnant and looking to give her child up for adoption.

But Louis Liotti did not recall the woman's correct name and offered little that would help his son trace her. And within a year of Louis Liotti's life-shaking revelation to his son, both he and his wife had died.

It was then that Liotti, who is married with three adult children, set out on a quest, petitioning to open his file in the Nassau County Surrogate's Court and hiring a private investigator to uncover details about his adoptive parents and why they had given him up.

As Liotti began to question all things in his past, including his spiritual beliefs, he even consulted a channeler, he said. The channeler said he believed Liotti's birth father had been a lawyer, and that there had been a scandal in the family.

But none of the information the channeler offered could be confirmed, and Liotti was still left wanting.

At last, Liotti gained access to his court file and found out his birth mother's name: Anne Ferguson.

He gave her name to an investigator and was able to learn only the barest framework of her life: That she was of Irish descent, about 35 when she gave birth. She had moved to Port Washington in 1977 and lived there — just minutes from Liotti's Westbury home, until 1997, when she moved to Cleveland. She died in 2000, Liotti said.

Liotti never learned his birth father's name, but he believes he may have been English.

Liotti's youngest daughter, Francesca, said her father was deeply affected by his search for identity.

Thomas Liotti, in his Garden City law office, looks at photographs of his parents Eileen Liotti and

NEWSDAY, SUNDAY, JANUARY 29, 2012   www.newsday.com

DEC cited on runoff

BY ROBERT BRODSKY
robert.brodsky@newsday.com

Long Island environmental advocates yesterday hailed a state court ruling that found the Department of Environmental Conservation has failed to properly oversee municipal stormwater runoff, considered a top cause of beach closures and waterway pollution.

In a ruling unsealed last week, Westchester Supreme Court Justice Joan Lefkowitz found the DEC's process for regulating stormwater did not comply with the federal Clean Water Act and must be revised.

When it rains, pollutants from streets, rooftops and chemically treated lawns flow into sewer systems, which then drain into local waterways.

The result, said Kevin McAllister, president of Peconic Baykeeper, a nonprofit that monitors Long Island waterways, are

beaches and shellfish beds contaminated with bacteria.

"Stormwater runoff has been a big problem when you consider the suburbanization of Long Island," he said.

Environmental groups, led by the Natural Resources Defense Council, filed suit against the state in June 2010, arguing that its permit process failed to reduce urban runoff.

The state issues one permit to each municipality — with the exception of New York City, which has its own oversight process — allowing them to self-certify their stormwater pollution control measures.

"One size does not fit all with these permits," McAllister said. "Southold will have different issues than Huntington."

Lefkowitz ordered the state to rewrite the permit to include more oversight, stricter compliance with schedules to reduce runoff and more public partici-

pation in permit hearings.

The DEC is "reviewing the decision and determining our next steps," said spokeswoman Charalessa King.

Environmental advocates contend that reducing stormwater runoff will also have an economic impact on Long Island. The Natural Resources Defense Council has found urban runoff is the leading cause of beach closings and advisories, costing Long Island more than $60 million in 2007.

"Stormwater is certainly a major problem," said James Ammerman, director of New York Sea Grant. "Anything we can do to deal with it is a good thing."

John German, president of the Long Island Sound Lobsterman's Association, said stormwater reduction measures have left water too sterile. "It's about developing an eco-management system," he said. "If you do one thing, it affects another."

Louis Liotti, who adopted him.

"For my dad, I can imagine feeling confused, finding out his biological mother was living a few towns away from us throughout his whole life," said Francesca Liotti, 22.

Even before his parents died, Thomas Liotti made peace with their decision to keep his adoption a secret, and felt grateful to them more than anything else.

Liotti said his father, during his last days alive, apolo-

gized for the rush way he had revealed the adoption.

"He said, 'That was when the devil was in me.' " Liotti said, adding that his father encouraged him to write the book. Liotti, in turn, said he did his best to thank his adoptive father in the last days of his life.

"They devoted their whole lives to me, a stranger," Liotti said. "I tried to articulate how much I loved him and how grateful I was."

NOW ONLINE
See photos of Thomas Liotti. newsday.com/li

Hundreds answer call to help girl

BY KERY MURAKAMI
kery.murakami@newsday.com

While 8-year-old Kaitlyn Rochel lay battling leukemia in New York University Medical Center, nearly a thousand people converged on Wantagh High School yesterday, hoping to save her life or someone else's.

For the second time, the Wantagh girl needs a bone-marrow transplant to combat the cancer she's fought since she was 3.

In the school gymnasium, where a sign read "House of the Warriors," Jonathan Szuguia was among a steady stream of people who had their cheeks swabbed to see if they were a match to be a donor.

It took only a few minutes to spur what Kaitlyn's family hopes will lead to a long life of memories. "I want to save someone's life if I can," said the Seaford resident, who like many tested, never met the girl.

Kaitlyn's mother, Carolyn, 28, wore a T-shirt with her two daughters' pictures on it, and took in the crowd, overwhelmed by the outpouring. Someone in the room might save her daughter's life.

Kaitlyn had been diagnosed with leukemia, which is caused by unhealthy bone marrow, when she was 3. In 2010,

Carolyn Rochel's daughter Kaitlyn was diagnosed with leukemia at 3. Potential bone marrow donors were tested yesterday.

her younger sister, Lauren, now 6, donated her bone marrow to Kaitlyn. The family believed the ordeal was over.

Last fall, the cancer returned. "It was devastating," Rochel said, tearing as she recalled Kaitlyn's reaction: " 'Why me? Why does this have to happen again?' "

Chemotherapy resumed. With her immune system compromised by radiation, Kaitlyn has been hospitalized. "She misses playing soccer. She misses being in school," Rochel said. She misses playing dolls at home with Lauren.

Her doctors have said she needs a marrow transplant, hopefully by March, Rochel said. If no donor is found by

then, she said, "it's not good."

Only four in 10 people needing a bone-marrow transplant find one in time, said Erika Toto, a donor coordinator for DKMS, an international bone marrow donation group that is testing the swabs. Other potential donors can be mailed home testing kits through dkmsamericas.org/register.

Debbie Amato of Farmingdale was volunteering at a bake sale at the school to help DKMS pay for processing the swabs. Joining her was her 9-year-old son, Jake, who received a bone-marrow transplant in 2010. So far, the cancer hasn't returned.

"Jake is here because somebody got swabbed," Amato said.

(L to R) Richard Ferguson (grandfather); Anna Erwin (1st Cousin); Eileen Ferguson (Aunt); Anne Ferguson (TFL's mother); Ellen Erwin Ferguson (grandmother)

Printed in the United States
By Bookmasters